Rosie's Riveting Recipes

Comfort Food & Kitchen Wisdom
from 1940s America

DANIELA TURUDICH

STREAMLINE PRESS

Published by Streamline Press
www.streamlinepressshop.com

First Edition
ISBN 978-1-930064-17-1

Other fine books from Streamline Press are available from your local bookstore or direct from the publisher.

The images contained within this book were sourced from the National Archive, Library of Congress.

EVERY EFFORT HAS BEEN MADE to trace and acknowledge all copyright holders. Streamline Press and the author would like to apologize if any credit omissions have been inadvertently made. If brought to our attention, we will gladly make changes to any subsequent editions.

Distributed to the book trade by IPG, Chicago.

Table of Contents

I'm Proud... my husband wants me to do my part

SEE YOUR U. S. EMPLOYMENT SERVICE
WAR MANPOWER COMMISSION

I'm proud ... my husband wants me to do my part
Howitt, John Newton
National Archive, Library of Congress

Author's Note

Trying to feed a family with limited time and a limited budget is daunting. For me, most of the recipes in cookbooks, on cooking shows, and online sounded truly amazing until I had to purchase all of the ingredients in order to make them. To try a new recipe, often meant spending more than I wanted for an ingredient, spending several hours time, and then feeling like an idiot in the kitchen.

I'm not a chef by any means – but I am a pretty good cook (at least according to my husband). Still, I often felt like I was missing the basics. "Elevating" food was great … but was I missing a step? Did I really need to go to culinary school to learn how to cook more simply?

So I revolted. I wanted to move away from what seemed to me like overly complicated methods and recipes. I wanted to feel comfortable in the kitchen without feeling like I needed to become a "chef" or a foodie – and I didn't want to feel embarrassed for wanting to cook more simply.

So … I started researching about how women used to cook. This yearn for simpler recipes – led me to an enormous amount of kitchen wisdom and cooking methods that have been somewhat discounted and lost to the ages.

Our grandmothers knew a thing or two about how to feed a family on a budget and how to stretch available food resources into wholesome and nutritious meals. "Waste not, want not"was the theme of the day – and I wanted to bring this theme back.

Rosie's Riveting Recipes is meant to be a collection of recipes used by women who labored and worked full time in factories during the day – but were still expected to provide healthy, nutritious meals for their family. It wasn't just expected – it was their wartime duty.

~ Daniela Turudich

Food and 1940s America

1940s America changed the way we lived. Coming out of the Great Depression into a World War affected the mindset and the choices of Americans and forever changed the American diet.

As the US entered the war, Americans at war and on the home front were faced with a few challenges. First, World War II was one of the largest transfers of labor in US history. Millions left for service and the war demanded food to feed them. Key foods, especially those that could keep well, had more nutrients, or were more amenable to factory methods went towards feeding the armed forces.

Second, money was in short supply. With the traditional "bread winner" now at war, wartime price hikes, and the rationing of foods and other items, people had to make the best use of what they could get. Home front Americans were asked to replace preferred foods like meat, sugar, and butter with substitutes, grow their own food, or do without.

Many of the recipes in this book can be done straight as printed or adapted to use ingredients you are more comfortable with. The recipes are meant to showcase a simpler method of cooking – that stretched available foods while providing much needed nutrients for a growing and working family.

Prior to delving into the recipes, we'd like to give you an overview of the choices and changes that homemakers were faced with in feeding their families. In this section you will find…
-- Uncle Sam's Daily Food Rules
-- Key foods that were rationed and how rationing affected the American diet.
-- Wartime "basic necessities" that every cook would have had on hand.
-- Sugar substitutes.
-- Butter extenders and substitutes.
-- Chocolate substitutes.
-- Meat substitutes equal to a serving of meat as a source of protein.

Uncle Sam's Daily Food Rules (1943)

Rule 1:
Milk and Milk Products
At least a pint for everyone—more for children—
or cheese or evaporated dry milk.

Rule 2:
Oranges, Tomatoes (and Tomato Juice), Grapefruit—
or raw cabbage or salad greens
At least one of these.

Rule 3:
Green or Yellow Vegetables (fresh, canned, or quick frozen)
One big helping or more, some raw, some cooked.

Rule 4:
Other Vegetables, Fruits (fresh, dried, canned, or quick frozen)
Potatoes, other vegetables or fruits in season.

Don't let pretty labels on cans mislead you, but learn the difference between grades and the relative economy of buying larger instead of small cans. The Pure Food Law requires packers to state exact quantity and quality of canned products, so take advantage of this information and buy only after thorough inspection of labels.
1942 | Rosener, Ann
National Archive, Library of Congress

Rule 5:
Bread and Cereal
Whole grain products or enriched white bread or flour.

Rule 6:
Meat, Poultry, or Fish
Dried beans, peas, or nuts occasionally.

Rule 7:
Eggs
At least 3 or 4 a week, cooked as you choose—or in "made" dishes.

Rule 8:
Butter and Other Spreads (including margarine) or
vitamin rich fats, peanut butter, and similar spreads.

Then eat other foods you also like.

Why greases must be saved. A soldier of the home front--and there's one in every American kitchen--saves all waste fats and greases so that they can be processed into ammunition for America's soldiers on the battlefronts. Pan and broiler drippings, deep fats, renderings from bacon rinds, these are some of the fats which should be put through a strainer to remove meat scraps and other solids, and poured into wide-mouthed cans such as coffee or fat cans.
1942 | Rosener, Ann
National Archive, Library of Congress

What was rationed?

Among other things, the following items were rationed:

Butter
Sugar
Oil
Red Meat

Wartime diets changed to include:

More eggs
More cheese
More grains
More chicken
More fish
Less red meat

People were urged to...

Extend meals containing minimal available meat with grains and fiber.
Stretch and substitute butter with margarine.
Substitute sugar with molasses or honey.
Make stews.
Eat more fruits and vegetables.
Grow their own fruits and vegetables (Victory Garden).
Can excess food.
Eat salads.
Make vegetables, eggs, cheese, and grains center stage.

Paying attention to the nutritional value in food was of utmost importance. People were expected to make sure they were getting the most vitamins, minerals, and energy from available foods to ensure they were strong and healthy for wartime work.

Wartime Basic "Necessities"

To help extend limited foods and to add more flavor to meals, many recipes called for "white sauce" and French dressing. These were very popular mealtime staples during the war years. We've provided master recipes for both that can be used when recipes contained within the book call for a white sauce or French dressing.

Wartime White Sauce (Cream Sauce)

Butter or oil
Flour
Milk
Salt and pepper to taste

Melt in pot 2 tablespoons butter or other fat. Add 2 tablespoons flour and mix thoroughly. Cook flour in fat, stirring constantly, until flour is slightly browned (this is your roux). Remove from heat and whisk in 2 cups milk. Return to heat and stir constantly until mixture thickens. Cook a few minutes more if there is a raw starch taste to the sauce. Season with salt and pepper to taste.

White sauce can be made thinner or thicker by adjusting the amount of milk added to the roux.

Victory Cheese Sauce

Follow the directions for wartime white sauce and add 1 cup of shredded cheese to mixture after you have whisked the milk into the roux. You may need to add more milk if the sauce become too thick.

Victory French Dressing

You can use this dressing generously for your salad greens without adding ration points.

½ cup salad oil
¼ cup lemon juice
¼ cup water
¾ teaspoon salt
¼ cup ketchup
1 ½ teaspoons granulated sugar
1 teaspoon bottled horse radish
1 ¼ teaspoon prepared mustard
½ teaspoon paprika
1 peeled garlic clove
½ teaspoon Worcestershire sauce

Combine all the ingredients in a covered jar, and shake well. Store in refrigerator, and use as needed, shaking well before using. Makes 1 1/3 cups.

Women in industry. Tool production. Sharp eyes and agile fingers make these young women ideal machine operators. They're conditioning and reshaping milling cutters in a huge Midwest drill and tool company. Republic Drill and Tool Company, Chicago, Illinois.
1942 | Rosener, Ann
National Archive, Library of Congress

Sugar Substitutes

During wartime, sugar was rationed. Women either didn't make sweets, or substituted sugar for other sweeteners. Some of these are listed below.

Honey

Honey can be substituted for sugar in desserts, cakes, cookies, vegetables, salad dressings, fruits, preserves, breads and candies. It is not satisfactory in Angel Food and Sponge cake.

The sweet content is equivalent to that of sugar. It has a flavor that is difficult to disguise. Bland varieties, light in color, are least highly flavored and therefore best for cooking. If granulation occurs, place container in hot water until crystals are melted.

When using honey for baking, honey adds moisture so be sure the cake is well baked. Additionally, it is not advisable to use honey in both the cake and the frosting. The flavor is too pronounced.

Corn Syrup

Like honey, corn syrup can be substituted for sugar in desserts, cakes, cookies, vegetables, salad dressings, fruits, preserves, breads and candies. It is not satisfactory in Angel Food and Sponge cake.

Maple Syrup

Maple syrup is good as a sweetening agent. It can be used in sauces and recipes adapted to its use, where a mild maple flavor is desired.

Molasses

Molasses is rich in iron as well as flavor. It doesn't make for the best sugar substitute but is satisfactory as a sweetening agent.

When a recipe calls for 1 cup granulated sugar, you may substitute the following…

	Honey	**Corn Syrup**	**Maple Syrup**	**Molasses**
Amount	1 cup – reduce liquid by ¼	1 cup – reduce liquid by 1/3	1 ¼ cups – reduce liquid by ½	1 cup
When used in baking – (acidity)	Add 1/8 teaspoon baking soda for each cup (or no soda)	Add 1/8 teaspoon baking soda for each cup (or no soda)	Add ¼ teaspoon baking soda for each cup	Add ½ teaspoon baking soda for each cup
For comparable sweetness	¾ cup equal 1 cup granulated sugar	2 cups equal 1 cup granulated sugar	1 ½ cups equal 1 cup granulated sugar	1 ½ cups equal 1 cup granulated sugar
Miscellaneous Notes	Thickness of honey must be taken into consideration in any substitution	Good in custards, muffins, drop cookies, cakes, frostings and in preserved fruits	Good on cereals, in puddings, and in sauces	Cakes will be heavier but stay moist longer

Norma Jean Dougherty (Marilyn Monroe) working at an airplane facotry in Van Nuys, Calif.
1944 | Conover, David
National Archive

Butter Extenders and Substitutes

During the war, butter was rationed and scarce. Most of it was kept for the table as a table spread and extended with additional ingredients.

Methods of Extending Butter

These are recommended as spreads but are not adapted to frying, greasing pans or to recipes unless especially designed for their use.

Basic Butter Extender

1 part cream
4 parts butter
Have butter soft, at room temperature, before combining with cream. Beat with an electric mixer 5 minutes at slow speed, then 5 minutes at high speed. Chill.

Victory Spread

Place ½ pound (1 cup) each butter and margarine in warm bowl. Cream until soft but not oily. Gradually add 1 cup lukewarm milk, beating with an electric mixer until mixture is well blended. Add salt to taste. Store in tightly covered dishes in refrigerator.

Butter Plus +

Soften 1 tablespoon (1 envelope) unflavored gelatin in ¼ cup cold milk; dissolve over boiling water. Add 1 ¾ cups lukewarm milk. Cream 1 pound (2 cups) butter in warm bowl, beating in gelatin-milk with an electric mixer until mixture is well blended. Add salt to taste. Store in tightly covered dishes in refrigerator. Use for seasoning vegetables, spreads, but not as a substitute for shortening.

4 to 1 Butter Spread

1 pound butter
2 pounds margarine
1 tall can evaporated milk

Allow both butter and margarine to reach room temperature, then break up, place in mixing bowl and add 1 teaspoon salt. Blend together, then gradually mix in evaporated milk. When thoroughly blended, form into squares, or pack in loaf pan, wrap securely in wax paper and store in the refrigerator. This will make 4 pounds of butter spread.

Butter Substitutes

For sautéing …
Cooks used salad oil, margarine, vegetable shortening, lard, or drippings. Bacon or sausage drippings and chicken and meat fat were saved and stored in the refrigerator and used for sautéing.

For baking cakes and cookies …
Cooks used margarine and vegetable shortening in place of butter.

Margarine

Margarine can be substituted for butter in all recipes, though the flavor may be slightly different. It is improved by creaming. Bring to room temperature, beat vigorously, add a little salt and place in refrigerator to harden.

Saving and Clarifying Fats – Wartime Style

Don't discard cooking fats. Fat can be clarified by heating with raw potato. Use about 4 slices per quart of fat. When fat bubbles and potato slices are brown, strain into a jar through 2 or 3 thicknesses of cheese cloth, placed over wire strainer. The potato absorbs any undesirable flavor.

Chocolate Substitute

Cocoa

As a substitute for chocolate, use 3 tablespoons cocoa plus ½ tablespoon shortening for each square of chocolate. When baking, sift with dry ingredients.

Cocoa can be used in cakes, cookies, desserts, sauces, frostings, candies, etc.

Drilling a wing bulkhead for a transport plane at the Consolidated Aircraft Corporation plant, Fort Worth, Texas.
Oct. 1942 | Hollem, Howard R.
National Archive, Library of Congress

Mary Louise Stepan, 21, used to be a waitress. She has a brother in the air corps. She is working on transport parts in the hand mill, Consolidated Aircraft Corp., Fort Worth, Texas.
Oct. 1942 | Hollem, Howard R.
National Archive, Library of Congress

Equal to a Serving of Meat as a Source of Protein
(1943)

1. A serving of fish, shellfish, poultry, game, or a variety of meat, such as liver, kidney, heart, etc.
2. Two medium eggs, cooked in any way.
3. One pint milk – whole, skim, or buttermilk.
4. About 3 oz. (6 tablespoons) cottage cheese.
5. About 2 oz. (1/2 c. grated) American cheese.
6. Four tablespoons peanut butter. At this meal include a milk dessert or milk to drink.
7. About ¾ cup cooked soybeans.
8. About ¾ to 1 cup cooked dried peas, beans, or lentils, as baked beans, chili beans, cooked limas, etc.
9. One cup of a cereal main dish such as macaroni and cheese or cheese fondue, 2 slices French toast, etc.

    Reminder: In serving dried beans or peas or lentils, or cereal products such as bread, breakfast cereals, macaroni, as a meat alternative, do one of two things: 1. Choose a dish in which dried beans or peas or lentils or a cereal product are combined with a small amount of one or 2. more of high-quality-protein foods such as milk, cheese, eggs, fish, meat, or poultry.

    Additionally: If you're serving a bean or cereal dish that does not contain one of the foods mentioned above, as baked beans, be sure to include in the meal a milk or milk-and-egg dessert, or a milk drink, or cheese in salad, or cheese and crackers for dessert.

10. If the Victory garden provides you with a vegetable dinner, be sure your dessert is made from milk (as rennet custard dessert) or from milk and egg, or milk and cereal, or a milk, cereal, and egg dessert (as bread or rice pudding).
11. If you're having generous bowls of a hearty soup as the main dish, serve a salad of tossed greens, vegetables or fruit, and a dessert that will step up the protein of the meal – Spanish cream, cream pie, or one of the desserts in No. 10.
12. A main-dish salad in which vegetables and a small amount of meat, fish, eggs, or poultry have been combined with macaroni, rice or some cubed potatoes may be your choice. In this case, round out the protein of the meal with one of the desserts in Nos. 10 or 11.

Soups & Salads

Production. Aircraft engines. A veteran of the assembly bench, twenty-two-year-old Anne Weinmen, employee of a large Midwest aircraft factory, inspects pistons to be used in airplane engines. With several years experience in Midwestern plants behind her, Miss Weinmen has developed the patience and dexterity this work requires. Melrose Park, Buick plant.
Rosener, Ann
National Archive, Library of Congress

Soups

Victory Soup Pot

2 cups sifted flour
½ teaspoon salt
1 egg, well beaten
6 cups chicken or beef broth

Combine flour, salt and beaten egg and blend until mixture is crumbly. Pour into boiling broth and cook 10 minutes. The rivels will look like boiled rice when cooked. Serves 8.

A Wartime Soup Pot

For thrifty soups or stock, save all the meat trimmings and left-over pieces of cooked meat and fowl, bones, vegetables, broth, gravy, liquid from cooked vegetables, and trimmings from lettuce, celery, or other vegetables. These will keep fresh in the refrigerator several days. Add sliced onions, chopped carrots, minced beef or some bouillon cubes. Add extra water or tomatoes for liquid as needed. Simmer until all ingredients are tender, adding rice, barley, or cubes of potatoes, and salt, pepper, herbs, and other desired seasonings during the last ½ hour of cooking. Remove bones and serve.

Women war workers.
1942 | Palmer, Alfred T.
National Archive, Library of Congress

Low-Ration-Point Stew

1 pound ground beef
3 slices bread soaked in milk, salt, pepper, and onion juice
¼ cup fat
2 tablespoons flour
1 tablespoon chili sauce (may omit)
1 cup tomato soup or soup stock
2 cups hot water

Dumpling Mixture

Season meat well with salt, pepper, and onion juice. Add soaked bread. Shape lightly into small cakes. Place fat in deep stew pan, put cakes and brown on all sides.

Lift out cakes and add 2 cups hot water, chili sauce, tomato soup, salt to taste. Thicken with flour (that has been mixed in cold water to form a paste). Replace cakes in saucepan. Simmer for 15 minutes. Drop dumpling mixture on top of meat cakes, cover loosely, and cook 15 minutes on top of stove, or 20 minutes in hot oven at 400° F. For quick and easy dumplings, use prepared biscuit mix according to package instructions.

Frances Eggleston, aged 23, came from Oklahoma, used to do office work. Consolidated Aircraft Corp., Fort Worth, Texas
Oct. 1942 | Hollem, Howard R.
National Archive, Library of Congress

There's no June in January for the housewife with economy and Victory on her mind. Buying foods out of season means less food for more money, and less money available for household staples and defense stamps.
Rosener, Ann
National Archive, Library of Congress

Wartime Bean, Pea or Lentil Soup

1 cup dried beans, peas or lentils
4 cups cold water
Ham bone, turkey carcass, or bacon rind OR 2 oz salt pork
1 medium onion
1 stalk celery
1 whole clove
1 bay leaf
1 teaspoon salt
Dash of pepper

Pick over, wash, cover well with water, and let beans soak overnight. In the morning, measure water and add enough to make 4 cups, if necessary. Combine all ingredients in the soup pot. Cover and simmer for 2 hours, or until beans, peas or lentils are soft. Drain, reserve liquid. Remove meat and chop or puree vegetables. Combine with liquid and add any additional seasonings desired. Reheat and serve with crackers.

Combine for Flavor

Bean Soup: Chili powder and parsley; sage and celery tops; or paprika and nutmeg. Serve with bits of boiled bacon, lemon slices, diced hard-cooked egg, or parsley.
Pea Soup: Use carrot and a little onion; or mustard and paprika. Serve with grated carrots, thinly sliced frankfurts, minced ham, chives or parsley.
Lentil Soup: Use lemon juice and celery salt; chili powder; or sage. Serve with slices of hard-cooked egg, lemon, or grated cheese.

Patriotic Fish Soup

If boiled fish is served for a meal keep a quart of the water and use the next day as a soup base with flaked left-over fish.

3 cups fish stock
1 cup flaked fish
½ teaspoon onion juice
1 sprig parsley
1 tablespoon butter
1 tablespoon flour
1 cup milk
Salt to taste

Remove all the skin and bones from fish. Mash with the back of a spoon gradually adding water, onion juice, salt. Melt the butter in a pot, blend in the flour and milk. The turn in the fish and let cook 15 minutes. When serving sprinkle with chopped parsley.

Tom Sawyer Fish Stew

If the day's catch is scant – clean fish, filleting large ones; then deep-sea them in traditional army style: melt 2 tablespoons bacon or other fat in skillet. Put in layer sliced raw potatoes, place fish on this and cover with sliced onions; add layer of whole unsalted soda crackers; top with more potatoes. Season each layer with salt, black pepper and butter. Add small amount of water, cover tightly, simmer about 45 minutes or until most of liquid has evaporated. Add top milk to almost cover; cook 5 minutes longer. (for 6 servings use 6 medium potatoes, 4 onions, and 1 to 1 ½ pounds fish fillets.)

Carrot Cream Soup

1 large raw potato
2 medium carrots
1 sliced, peeled medium onion
½ minced, peeled medium clove garlic
½ cup broth
¾ teaspoon salt
2 tablespoon butter or margarine
2 tablespoon flour
⅛ teaspoon pepper
1 ½ cups milk or ¾ cup evaporated milk mixed with ¾ cup water

Cut potato and carrots in thin slices without paring. Cook in a covered saucepan with onion, garlic, broth, and ½ teaspoon salt for 10 minutes or until tender. Remove and press through sieve. Make a white sauce using the butter, flour, remaining salt, pepper and milk. Stir in carrot mixture. Heat. Serves 4. Serve with lettuce, dried beef and mayonnaise sandwiches, and melon for lunch.

Potato Soup

1 cup milk
3 potatoes
3 leeks or 3 onions
2 or 3 tablespoons celery, chopped
2 cups water or chicken stock
½ teaspoon salt

Cut potatoes, onion and celery, and place in water on stovetop. Add salt and cook about ½ hour, or until soft. Drain, making sure to retain the soup. Add 1 or 2 cups of milk to soup and bring to boil. Thicken soup with cornstarch (first mixed with water). Dice potato, leeks, and celery and add back to soup, if desired.

Parsley Soup

2 cups milk
1 cup water or chicken broth
2 egg yolks
1 teaspoon salt
2 tablespoons butter or margarine
2 tablespoons flour
1 medium onion (whole)
Bouillon cub (if available)
1 tablespoon lemon juice
½ cup cream
½ cup parsley, finely chopped

Melt butter in soup pot. Add flour and salt and liquids and onion. Simmer for 1 hour. Remove onion and add cream mixed with yolk of two eggs. Cook until thickened. Just before serving add parsley. Stir well and serve at once.

Conservation of durable goods. So-o-o-o big! But still not quite big enough to sell to the junk man or give to the Red Cross, Boy Scouts or other agencies in the neighborhood. Conservation of waste paper will save millions of dollars annually for Uncle Sam. When that pile is broomstick high, they'll be a hundred pounds of essential paper.
Feb. 1942 | Rosener, Ann
National Archive, Library of Congress

Whole Wheat Chowder

2 cups cooked whole wheat
2 cups diced carrots, cooked
½ cup diced salt pork
4 tablespoons chopped onion
1 tablespoon flour
1 pint milk
1 teaspoon salt
Pepper
1 tablespoon chopped parsley

In a soup pot, fry the salt pork until crisp and remove it from the fat. Fry onion in remaining fat until yellow. Add flour to onion in frying pan and cook a few minutes longer. Add all other remaining ingredients (except parsley) to soup pot over low heat, stirring until well blended. Cook for about 10 minutes, stirring occasionally. Sprinkle parsley over chowder at the end of cooking.

Production. Aircraft engines. That little instrument Verna Lampy is wielding looks and sounds a lot like the drill your third bicuspid may be familiar with. It's used in a huge Midwest aircraft plant, however, to etch serial and inspection numbers on airplane motor parts, making a permanent record to facilitate assembly and production count. Melrose Park, Buick plant.
Jul. 1942 | Rosener, Ann
National Archive, Library of Congress

Salads

Victory Garden Salad

½ head lettuce
1 cup diced celery
2 fresh tomatoes
3 hard cooked eggs
1 clove garlic
1 cucumber
½ bunch radishes
French dressing (see recipe on page 50)

Shred lettuce; dice celery, cut tomatoes in small pieces; and slice radishes.
Also cut eggs and cucumbers in cubes. Rub salad bowl with clove of garlic (assumes you are using a wooden salad bowl). Toss salad together then marinate for 1 hour in French dressing. Drain. Mix with mayonnaise. Serve in large salad bowl, garnished with hard cooked eggs, sliced radishes and parsley.

Wartime Note: The vegetables must be washed lightly, dried, and stored covered in your refrigerator long enough to crisp before using.

War gardens for victory--Grow vitamins at your kitchen door / lithographed by the Stecher-Traung Lithograph Corporation, Rochester, New York.
Date Created/Published: [between 1939 and 1945]
National Archive, Library of Congress

Eggplant Salad

1 eggplant
4 tomatoes, cut into quarters or eighths
1 tablespoon chopped parsley
Thyme, wine vinegar
Olive oil, salt, pepper
Garlic clove

Bake the eggplant in a moderate oven for about an hour. Remove and peel; dice eggplant and place in a salad bowl that has been previously rubbed with the garlic clove. Add the tomatoes and sprinkle in parsley and thyme. Make a dressing of oil, vinegar, salt and pepper. Allow the salad to marinate for awhile so that the vegetables may take on the flavor of seasonings.

Victory Potato Salad

Boil, peel and cool potatoes. When cold, cut into thin slices or cubes. Arrange in a dish, add salt, pepper, minced onion and minced celery. Pour olive oil and vinegar over all and stir carefully. You may also add thinly sliced sour apples and hard boiled eggs.

Apple and Grape Salad

Chop apples into tiny cubes. Mix in halved, peeled seedless grapes. Mix with thinned mayonnaise and surround with watercress.

French Spinach Salad

½ pound uncooked spinach
1 medium sweet onion, minced
4 tablespoons diced celery
4 hard-cooked eggs, sliced
¾ cup lemon salad dressing (see recipe page on 50)
Salt to taste

Chill salad ingredients and toss together lightly. Add lemon salad dressing just before serving. Serves 8.

Macaroni and Egg Salad

¼ cup macaroni in 1 inch pieces
3 cup boiling water
1 teaspoon salt
6 tablespoon French dressing (see recipe on page 50)
1 ½ cups coarsely shredded carrots
½ teaspoon celery salt
2 tablespoon mayonnaise
2 shelled, hard cooked eggs
Shredded salad greens

Cook macaroni in boiling water with salt until tender. Drain; then combine with French dressing, and let stand until cool. Add carrots, celery salt, and mayonnaise, and mix thoroughly. Then add sliced eggs, and toss lightly. Serve on shredded greens, or toss shredded greens with salad ingredients. Serves 4. Variations:
1. Chopped parsley or watercress makes a nice addition to this salad and steps up the vitamin C.
2. Cold, leftover cooked vegetables may be substituted for the shredded carrots, if desired. This salad is nice with toasted whole wheat bread, strawberry preserves, and milk, for lunch.

This girl in a glass house is putting finishing touches on the bombardier nose section of a B-17F navy bomber, Long Beach, Calif. She's one of many capable women workers in the Douglas Aircraft Company plant. Better known as the "Flying Fortress," the B-17F is a later model of the B-17 which distinguished itself in action in the South Pacific, over Germany and elsewhere. It is a long range, high altitude heavy bomber, with a crew of seven to nine men, and with armament sufficient to defend itself on daylight missions.

Oct. 1942 | Palmer, Alfred T.
National Archive, Library of Congress

Sunny Homefront Salad

1 cup cooked peas
1 cup cooked green beans
1 cup sliced uncooked carrots
1 cup uncooked cauliflowerets
1 cup diced celery
French dressing (see recipe on next page)
6 large tomatoes
½ teaspoon salt
1 head lettuce
Mayonnaise
Parsley

Combine first 6 ingredients and chill. Peel tomatoes, sprinkle with salt, invert and chill. Drain tomatoes and cut each into 5 sections, leaving whole at stem end. Place each on lettuce cup, fill with vegetables and top each with mayonnaise and parsley.

Makes for a nice red and white Red Cross luncheon salad.

Dressings

Victory French Dressing

You can use this dressing generously for your salad greens without adding ration points.

½ cup salad oil
¼ cup lemon juice
¼ cup water
¾ teaspoon salt
¼ cup ketchup
1 ½ teaspoons granulated sugar
1 teaspoon bottled horse radish
1 ¼ teaspoon prepared mustard
½ teaspoon paprika
1 peeled garlic clove
½ teaspoon Worcestershire sauce

Combine all the ingredients in a covered jar, and shake well. Store in refrigerator, and use as needed, shaking well before using. Makes 1 1/3 cups.

Lemon Dressing

Use two teaspoons lemon juice, one-half cup oil, one teaspoon salt, black pepper. To this may be added a pinch of basil, a chopped egg, some chives.

Buttermilk Salad Dressing

This will solve the fat problem – either as to buying it or losing it!

2 tablespoons flour
½ teaspoon salt
¾ teaspoon dry mustard
2 ½ teaspoons sugar
Few grains cayenne
¾ cup buttermilk
1 egg lightly beaten
2 teaspoons butter or margarine
2 tablespoons vinegar

Combine flour, salt, mustard, sugar, and cayenne. Add 3 tablespoons buttermilk
and mix until smooth. Stir in remaining buttermilk and the egg. Cook over
hot water, stirring constantly until thickened. Remove from heat and stir in the
butter and vinegar. This dressing may be used for potato, Waldorf, or mixed green
vegetable salad.

Eggs & Cheese

Operating a hand drill at Vultee-Nashville, woman is working on a "Vengeance" dive bomber, Tennessee. Feb. 1943 | Palmer, Alfred T.
National Archive, Library of Congress.

Men and women make efficient operating teams on riveting and other jobs at the Douglas Aircraft plant, Long Beach, Calif. Most important of the many types of aircraft made at this plant are the B-17F ("Flying Fortress") heavy bomber, the A-20 ("Havoc") assault bomber and the C-47 heavy transport plane for the carrying of troops and cargo.
Oct. 1942 | Palmer, Alfred T.
National Archive, Library of Congress

Eggs

Wartime Soufflé (Basic)

3 tablespoons flour
2 tablespoons fat
1 cup milk
1 teaspoon salt
3 eggs (separated)
1 cup grated cheese or minced meat or vegetables or fruit

Melt fat in top of double boiler, stir flour in to make a smooth paste (roux). Add milk gradually and stir until mixture thickens. Add salt. This is your white sauce. Remove from fire and stir in egg yolks and material used for seasoning. Fold in stiffly beaten egg whites. Turn into greased baking dish and bake for 50 minutes at 325° F or until firm. Serve in dish in which it was baked; do not remove it from oven until it is to be served.

Wartime Tip: A husband who complains about left-overs served soufflé style is indeed rare. Try left-over minced ham, ground.

Eggs in Spinach Nest

Cover 6 eggs with cold water; bring to a boil, remove from heat; let stand covered 20 minutes. Meantime cook 2 pounds spinach in water, covered, 8 to 10 minutes. Drain; season. Now make mock hollandaise sauce: Place ¾ cup mayonnaise, ¼ teaspoon salt and a dash of pepper in top of double boiler, gradually stir in ⅓ cup water; cook covered over hot water about 5 minutes stirring constantly. Do not overcook. Arrange hot drained spinach and halved hot eggs. Pour mock hollandaise sauce over.

Deviled Eggs Garden Style

Cut 6 hard boiled eggs in half length wise. Remove the yolks and mash; to the yolks add mustard, salt, celery seed and mayonnaise to moisten; mix well. Refill whites. In a skillet melt 2 tablespoons fat, stir in 2 ½ tablespoons flour, ½ teaspoon chili powder; add 2 cups milk, ¼ teaspoon salt, and 1 bouillon cube (optional). Cook until thickened stirring constantly. Add 2 cups cut cooked green beans, asparagus or peas. Place eggs on sauce, cover tightly, reheat. Makes 6 servings.

Ring around my Dixie

A ring around scrambled eggs – served as a luncheon novelty.

1 onion, chopped
1 green bell pepper, chopped
2 tablespoons butter or fat
1 ½ cups canned tomatoes
Salt, Pepper
3 ½ cups cooked brown rice
1 ½ cups grated cheese
6 or more scrambled eggs

Cook onion and green pepper in fat; add tomatoes and rice; cook slowly over a low flame until rice has absorbed the liquid. Add seasonings and grated cheese.
Pack into a buttered ring mold; keep hot. Unmold the rice and fill the center with the scrambled eggs. Serves 6 to 8.

Egg Roll Call!

3 tablespoons margarine or shortening
3 tablespoons flour
¾ cup milk
1 teaspoon salt
6 hard cooked eggs
2 cups prepared biscuit mix
Milk to moisten

Make a thick white sauce of shortening, flour, milk, and salt. Add chopped hard cooked eggs. Cool.

Prepare biscuit dough, patting in oblong shape ¼ inch thick. Spread egg mixture on dough, roll up, jelly roll fashion. Cut into ½ inch slices.

Place on greased baking sheet; bake 15 minutes at 425° F. Serve with a cheese sauce. Cheese sauce can be made by making another white sauce and adding grated cheese to the sauce, stirring until melted.

Baked Sandwich Scramble

4 hard cooked eggs
½ cup grated cheese
2 tablespoons catsup
1 ½ cups well seasoned white sauce (made of fat, flour, milk and salt)
6 slices of bread, toasted

Heat white sauce; add grated cheese, catsup, chopped hard cooked eggs.
Place toast in oiled baking dish. Spread with filling.
Bake in moderate oven 350° F for 30 minutes. Garnish with paprika and salad greens.

De Land pool. Aircraft construction class. Women are being trained along with men in the Volusia County Florida Vocational School to take their places on the war production front. Susie Nelson, left, has a husband in Panama and a brother in the Navy. Pearl Kinchem, right, is a housewife with a brother in the army. Soon both of them will be welding aircraft in the De Land industrial pool.
Apr. 1942 | Hollem, Howard R.
National Archive, Library of Congress

Fluffy Omelet with Grains

½ cup bread crumbs
2 teaspoons salt
½ teaspoon pepper
½ cup milk
4 eggs
2 teaspoons fat

Soak the bread crumbs in milk for 15 minutes, then add salt and pepper. Separate the yolk and whites of the eggs and beat the whites until light.

Mix yolks with bread and milk. Cut in whites. Turn in heated oiled pan and cook until delicately brown around the edges. Place in a 350° F oven and bake until set and lightly brown. Fold and turn on heated dish.

Women in industry. Gas mask production. Flower in hair, Betty Gumbetter adds glamour to the assembly line of a Midwest gas mask factory which formerly made vacuum cleaners. Operating a riveting press, which attaches cloth tabs to the face pieces of gas masks, this young worker is one of the many company employees who switched over from work on vacuums when the plant was converted. Betty likes her new job better than the old one. "It bears a lot more relationship to my American Women's Voluntary Services work," she says. Eureka Vacuum, Detroit, Michigan.
July 1942 | Rosener, Ann
National Archive, Library of Congress

Cheese

Make-at-Home Cottage Cheese

1 quart milk
¼ cup sour or buttermilk
¼ rennet tablet
1 tablespoon cold water
Cream, salt
Heat milks in double boiler to room temperature (75° F). Remove from heat. Dissolve tablet in water and add to milk. Mix thoroughly. Cover with a cloth and stand in warm place 12 hours. Break curd, pour into cheesecloth-lined strainer and let drain thoroughly until dripping stops. Moisten with cream, season with salt and chill. Makes 1 cup.

Victory Cheese Custard

Put into a small saucepan 2 ounces grated cheese, 2 tablespoons cream or milk, 1 teaspoon prepared mustard, ½ teaspoon salt, and a little pepper, 2 beaten eggs, and a little thyme. Stir over fire until thick, then cool. Eat with bread.

Wartime Noodles and Cottage Cheese

Boil wide noodles (egg noodles) and drain. Add butter or margarine (to taste). Mix in generous amounts of cottage cheese and flavor with chives or horseradish. Can also omit chives and horseradish and season with salt, to taste.

Baked Bean and Cheese Loaf (Vegetarian)

½ onion, chopped
1 tablespoon fat
2 cups baked beans, drained
1 cup soft bread crumbs
2 eggs
2 tablespoons catsup
½ teaspoon salt
Few grains pepper
2 cups grated cheese

Brown onion in fat. Add mashed baked beans, bread crumbs, beaten eggs, catsup, salt, pepper, and cheese. Mix thoroughly.
Pack into greased loaf pan. Bake at 350° F about 45 minutes, or until firm. Serve hot with spicy tomato sauce or catsup. Serves 6.

Wartime Note: The generous amount of cheese gives this fine protein value. A real meat substitute!

Macaroni and Cheese Crisp

4 tablespoons fat
4 tablespoons flour
1 cup milk
1 teaspoon salt
1 cup grated yellow cheese
1 pimiento chopped (optional)
2 cup cooked macaroni
1 teaspoon grated onion
2 tablespoons chopped parsley

Make a white sauce of fat, flour, milk and salt.
Add grated cheese and stir until melted. Add rest of ingredients. Mix well. Pour into an oiled shallow pan. Chill.

Cut with a large biscuit cutter. Roll into beaten egg and fine bread crumbs.
Cook in 1 inch of hot fat until brown on both sides. Serves 4 to 6.

Cereal-Cheese Casserole

½ cup thinly sliced or minced onions
1 tablespoon fat or salad oil
2 cup chopped fresh tomatoes
2 teaspoon salt
Speck cayenne pepper
1 ½ teaspoon Worcestershire sauce
¾ cup brown whole grain cereal (such as cream of wheat or oatmeal)
2 cup boiling water
1 cup grated cheddar cheese (¼ pound)

Cook onions in fat until tender. Add tomatoes; then cover, and simmer for 10 minutes. Add ½ teaspoon. salt, cayenne pepper, and Worcestershire. Meanwhile, cook the cereal in boiling water with remaining salt for 3 to 5 minutes or as directed by manufacturer. Then arrange layers of cereal, tomatoes, onions, and cheese in a 1 quart casserole, with cheese as top layer. Bake in a moderately hot oven (400° F) for 20 minutes. Place under the broiler until the top is golden brown. Serves 4. It's nice with green beans, parsley cole slaw, heated rolls, iced melon, and tea for dinner.

"Gnocchi" with Cheese Sauce

A grand main dish for lunch or dinner
Cook ¾ cup quick-cooking wheat cereal in 3 cups boiling salted water 5 minutes, stirring frequently. Remove from heat, add ¼ cup margarine or butter and 2 slightly beaten egg yolks. Pour into greased shallow pan (about 8 x 8 inches) and let stand several hours or overnight. Cut into squares, place in a large shallow baking dish. Just before serving cover with a well-seasoned cheese sauce; sprinkle with grated cheese.

Place under broiler 10 minutes or until bubbling hot and delicately browned, or bake in a hot oven (450° F) 25 minutes.

Saucy Cheese Dumplings

Dumplings

2 cups flour
1 teaspoon salt
2 teaspoons double acting baking powder
½ cup shortening
⅔ cup milk
⅔ cup grated cheese

Tomato Sauce

3 tablespoons butter or fat
3 tablespoons chopped onion
3 tablespoons flour
3 cups canned tomatoes
½ teaspoon salt
⅔ teaspoon salt-pepper

Make sauce by melting butter, browning onion, adding flour and blending until smooth. Then add finely cut tomatoes and juice, and seasoning. Mix well. Bring to a boil before adding the dumplings.

Mix dry ingredients for dumplings. Add 2 tablespoons of the grated cheese, then shortening and blend in thoroughly.
Add milk and knead slightly to a round ball.
Roll out on floured board, to ⅛ inch thickness. Cut in 3 inch rounds and place 1 tablespoon grated cheese in the center of each. Wet edges with cold water, gather up like a bag, and pinch opening to seal.
Drop dumplings into tomato sauce. Cover tightly, steam 15 minutes without lifting cover. (Keep sauce simmering for steam enough to cook dumplings.) Serve hot.
Makes 10 dumplings, plenty of sauce.

Use prepared biscuit dough if you wish, it will save time.

Pointy Welsh Rabbit

1 tablespoon butter or fat
1 tablespoon flour
½ cup milk
Salt
½ teaspoon dry mustard
½ teaspoon Worcestershire sauce
½ pound sharp cheese, grated
Toast Points
Dash of cayenne

Make sauce of fat, flour, milk, and seasonings.
When thickened and smooth, add the shredded cheese. Stir until the cheese in melted, over very low heat.
Serve hot on toast points.

Manpower. Former actress now aircraft worker. From central casting to aircraft casting! Erstwhile child star of the silent picture days, auburn-haired Dorothy Langdon now inspects airplane engine parts in a Detroit war plant. Known as "Baby Dorothy Phelps" of the silents, and heart interest of western thrillers in the middle
thirties, Miss Langdon joined America's army of women war workers early this year. With a husband in the Army, the twenty-six-year-old beauty finds her new role in life eminently satisfying. "I'm really doing something," she says. "I got tired of just playing at doing something." In addition to her forty-eight hour work week at the inspection table, Miss Langdon still finds time to study drafting at night
July 1942 | Rosener, Ann
National Archive, Library of Congress

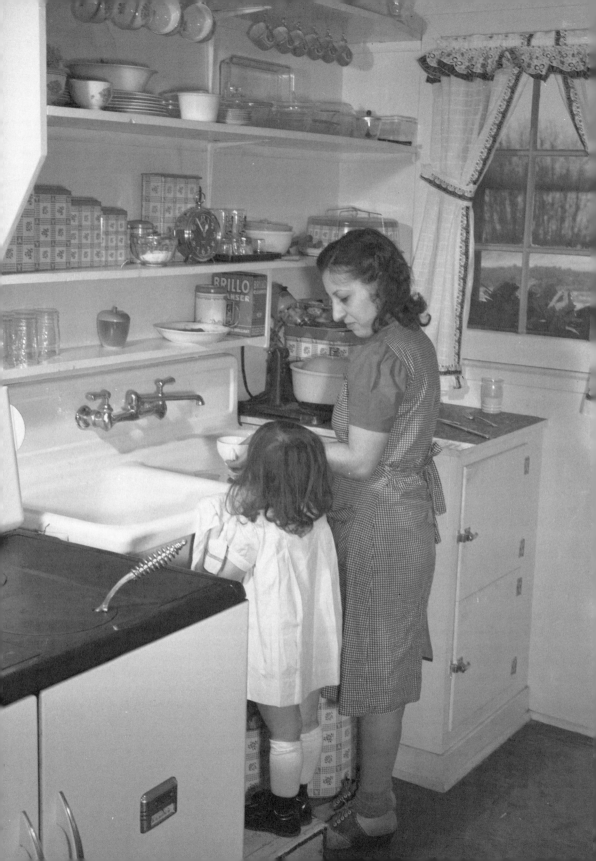

Fish

Bantam, Connecticut. Defense homes. Little Ann Heath is eager to try out all the facilities of her parents' new four-room defense housing unit, after spending most of her life in a single furnished room. Here she pushes her footstool to the sink in order to help her mother clean up the dinner dishes. Mrs. Heath, a native of Winsted, a city some twenty-five miles away, is delighted with her new kitchen--the first she's ever had which she actually considers as a kitchen, and is trying out all the recipes she has collected in five years of married life. The Heaths pay thirty dollars monthly for their apartment.
Jan. 1942 | Hollem, Howard R.
National Archive, Library of Congress

Conversion. Toy factory. From toy trains to parachute flare casings is the work history of Stephanie Cewe, whose skill with this electric screwdriver has been turned to the aid of Uncle Sam's war machine. Then Stephanie used to assemble toy locomotives; today, she uses the same screwdriver to assemble flare casings. A. C. Gilbert Company, New Haven, Connecticut.
Feb. 1942 | Hollem, Howard R.
National Archive, Library of Congress

Victory Fish Casserole

1 cup cooked flaked fish
1 cup white sauce
1 cup finely chopped nuts
2 hard cooked eggs, minced
Cracker crumbs
Butter or margarine

Combine fish, white sauce, nuts and eggs. Pour into a greased casserole and cover with cracker crumbs and dots of butter or margarine. Bake at 350° F for 25 minutes of until the crumbs are brown. Serves 4.

Finnan Haddie Vegetable Pie

2 tablespoons margarine
4 tablespoons flour
3 cups milk
Dash pepper
1 pound finnan haddie (smoked haddock)
1 cup diced onions
1 cup diced, cooked carrots
1 cup cooked peas
6 potatoes (mashed)

Make a thick cream sauce (white sauce made from roux) of the first 4 ingredients. Add finnan haddie (or any other smoked or soaked salt fish) cut crosswise into inch strips. Sauté onions in small amount of fat, add with carrots and peas to sauce; turn mixture into baking dish. Top with the mashed potatoes; brush with melted margarine. Bake in a hot oven (400° F) about 30 minutes.

Wartime Pan Fish

Flat fish
Cornmeal
Salt, lemon juice

Choose the best pan-fish your market offers; butterfish, sunfish, flounder, or porgy.
Have fishmonger remove head and tail, trim fins close, and if possible remove the
backbone. Mix salt with cornmeal, roll fish in it. Sauté fish in drippings (bacon
drippings are best) or other fat, till brown and crisp on both sides. Remove to hot
platter. Add 1 tablespoon boiling water to pan, a few drops of lemon juice; stir,
scraping the pan, pour over fish.

Wartime Fish Sauté

Fish steaks, filets, and small whole fish may be sautéed. Dust fish with salt, pepper
and flour. Or dip it in corn meal. Or in egg white and milk, then in breadcrumbs.
Have a heavy pan well heated and well greased, but do not have extra fat in the pan.
Cook the fish slowly, turning twice or more so that it browns evenly.

*Production. Willow Run bomber plant. Inspection of more than a thousand separate tubing pieces compos-
ing the fuel, hydraulic, de-icing and other systems in a bomber is a highly important job. This young employee at the giant Willow Run plant uses her tiny flashlight to discover any internal defects in the tubing.
Ford plant, Willow Run.
July 1942 | Rosener, Ann
National Archive, Library of Congress*

Wartime Boiled Fish

Fish is best boiled in court bouillon. If you have no fish boiler, place the fish on a plate; tie the plate securely, but loosely in cheesecloth, so that it can be removed from the boiling water without danger of breaking the fish. Simmer gently 6 to 10 minutes to 1lb. A thick chunk of fish or whole fish requires a longer time to cook though. Fish can be served hot with white sauce or cold with vegetable salad, cucumbers, lettuce and mayonnaise. Fish that lend themselves to being boiled, include:

Carp	Halibut
Cod	Mackerel
Eel	Salmon
Flounder	Sea Bass
Haddock	Shad
Hake	Whitefish

Court Bouillon

1 quart water
2 large onions, sliced
1 carrot, sliced
2 cloves
1 bay leaf
Fresh celery leaf – if any on hand
2 tablespoons vinegar
Salt and pepper
2 cloves of garlic, sliced

Simmer ingredients together for at least 15 minutes before adding fish, or the bouillon will have no flavor. If the vinegar is bitterly strong, use less. Taste.

Wartime Baked Fish

2 to 4 pounds of fish
Thin slices of salt pork
Salt and pepper
Fat
Lemon juice and lemon quarters
Chopped parsley

Place fish in well greased pan, skin side down (if half a fish). Put slices of salt pork over the fish and on the bottom of the pan. Bake at 400 to 450° F about 8 to 10 minutes to 1 lb. Remove to hot platter. Put 1 tablespoon of parsley in the pan, 2 to 3 tablespoons of boiling water, and a few drops of lemon juice. Stir them vigorously, scraping the pan. Pour this sauce over the fish. Garnish with lemon quarters. Serves 4-8.

Broiled Fish Fillets Piquante

2 pounds fish fillets like flounder or cod
1 tablespoon minced onion
¼ teaspoon pepper
1 to 2 tablespoons lemon juice
1 teaspoon salt
4 tablespoons melted butter or margarine
¼ teaspoon savory
¼ teaspoon marjoram
2 tablespoons minced parsley

Wash and dry fillets. Combine all remaining ingredients except parsley, and pour half of them into shallow pan. Lay fillets on top; then broil for 9 minutes – or until easily flaked with a fork – basting after 4 minutes. Arrange fillets on platter, and pour remaining sauce over them. Sprinkle with chopped parsley. If desired, medium tomatoes cut crosswise in thirds, sprinkled with salt and pepper and brushed with salad oil, can be broiled on broiler rack around fish, for the same length of time. Serves 6.

Agnes Cliemka, age 23, married and husband may be going into the service any day, Heil and Co., Milwaukee, Wisconsin. Agnes used to work in a department store. Checking of gasoline hose of gasoline trailers before being turned over the Air Force.
Feb. 1943 | Hollem, Howard R.
National Archive, Library of Congress

Left-Over Fish Gratin

2 cups fish
1 cup thick white sauce
½ cup grated cheese
¼ cup sherry
Breadcrumbs and butter or margarine
Lay left-over fish in casserole. Use sharp old cheese; add it to sauce; when it is thoroughly blended add sherry. Pour over fish. Put crumbs and butter or margarine on top, brown in a hot oven at 375° F for about 15 minutes. Serves 6-7. One pound of boiled fish may be substituted for left-over fish.

Left-Over Fish, Creamed

Flaked fish
White sauce

Heat sauce to boiling point; then reduce heat and add fish, forking it into the sauce; turn it over from time to time rather than stir, till thoroughly hot. Serve:

(1)   In a deep dish to hold the heat, minced parsley on top.
(2)   On toast sprinkled with paprika, or minced parsley, or minced chives, or chopped hard boiled egg, or bacon.
(3)   In a casserole gratin, with or without breadcrumbs and butter or margarine.
(4)   In a ring of leftover mashed potatoes.
(5)   In a deep casserole with a browned crust of left-over mashed potatoes. This is called Fish Pie.
(6)   Mixed with left-over rice and noodles.
(7)   Stuffed with breadcrumbs into green peppers and baked.

Canned Tuna and Tomatoes

1 can tuna fish
1 or 2 boiled eggs
3 or 4 fresh tomatoes

Make a good white sauce and add the broken up tuna fish and chopped hard boiled eggs. At the last minute dice the tomatoes and add. Serve with boiled rice. Salt and pepper to taste.

Canned Salmon and Sour Cream

1 can salmon
2 cups sour cream
Salt, pepper, lemon juice, mace

Remove fish, including the liquid, into a casserole. Stir the seasonings in the sour cream and pour it over the salmon. Bake slowly at 350° F, until cream is reduced to a thick sauce, with patches of brown on it – 20 to 30 minutes. Garnish with quartered lemon and serve with boiled potatoes, and green salad. Serves 5-6.

Men and women work side by side on the production lines at the Saint Louis, Missouri plant of the Airplane Division of the Curtiss-Wright Corporation. The male inspector in the rear checks the accuracy of the completed work of the women in the foreground.
Date Created/Published: [between 1935 and 1945]
National Archive, Library of Congress.

Conversion. Safety razor plant. Estelle Wilson, one of a New England razor factory's many women work-ers, checks completed V-blocks with blueprint specification. Because of their previous training, reading blueprints is no novelty to women employed in this plant which is now producing tool posts under subcon-tract. Gillette.
Feb. 1942 | Hollem, Howard R.
National Archive, Library of Congress

Scalloped Eggs and Shrimp

2 tablespoons butter or salad oil
2 tablespoons flour
½ teaspoon salt
1 cup milk
1 cup shrimp
4 eggs, hard cooked and sliced
½ cup bread crumbs

Make a white sauce of first 4 ingredients. Clean shrimp. In well-greased casserole arrange thin layers of white sauce, shrimp, eggs and crumbs. Brown in moderate oven at 350° F. Garnish the top with a few shrimp and serve hot. Serves 4.

Cucumber Sauce for Fish

1 cup cucumber
1 cup sour cream
½ teaspoon salt
¼ teaspoon mustard
Dash of pepper
1 tablespoon vinegar
1 teaspoon onion juice

Whip sour cream until it becomes thick. Mix cucumber, seasonings, onion juice and vinegar and stir into the cream. Beat just long enough to blend.

Bantam, Connecticut. War workers' homes. Fred Heath runs a turret lathe at the Warren McArthur plant, where he's been working since August 1941. He formerly worked in a machine shop in his native city Torrington. One of the first families to move into the new war workers' homes in Bantam, the Heaths, who have been married for five years, had previously been living in a furnished room in Torrington. Mrs. Heath formerly lived in Winsted, a town of about 25,000 people just a dozen miles from Torrington. They are proud of their new home and of the comfortable new furniture they bought on the installment plan in Torrington. They have besides the kitchen, a large living room, a modern bath, a medium-sized master bedroom and a smaller room for their three-year-old daughter, Ann.
Jan. 1942 | Hollem, Howard R.
National Archive, Library of Congress

Poultry

Victory Roast Chicken

Roasting chicken
Stuffing
Olive Oil
Salt and Pepper

Rinse chicken. Fill lightly with stuffing. Rub olive oil over chicken and dust with salt and pepper. Brown quickly in a hot oven 375-400° F; reduce heat to 350° F, cover tightly, and cook 12 – 15 minutes for each 1 lb of chicken.

Wartime Stuffing

1 ½ cups finely broken stale bread
1 cup diced celery
½ cup chopped onion
1 teaspoon salt
1 teaspoon paprika
2 tablespoons butter or margarine

Place in a large bowl the finely broken stale bread, and pour over it just enough boiling water to make the bread adhere in a dry dough. The place butter in a frying pan and when hot, put in the diced celery and chopped onion and fry together slowly until slightly browned; then add to the bread. Remove from heat and add salt and paprika. Mix thoroughly. Taste and adjust seasoning as necessary.

Working inside fuselage of a Liberator Bomber, Consolidated Aircraft Corp., Fort Worth, Texas. Oct. 1942 | Hollem, Howard R.
National Archive, Library of Congress

Women in industry. Tool production. Pioneers of the production line, these two young workers are among the first women ever to operate a centerless grinder, a machine requiring both the knowledge of precision measuring instruments, and considerable experience and skill in setting up. In this Midwest drill and tool plant, manned almost exclusively by women, centerless grinders have been efficiently operated by women for more than a year, and company production figures have continued to soar. Republic Drill and Tool Company, Chicago, Illinois.
Aug. 1942 | Rosener, Ann
National Archive, Library of Congress

Victory Chicken Pot Pie

3 cups diced, cooked chicken
1 cup diced cooked carrots
6 cooked small white onions
1 tablespoon chopped parsley
1 cup milk
1 cup chicken broth
2 tablespoons flour
1 teaspoon salt
1/8 teaspoon pepper

Arrange chicken, carrots, onions and parsley in layers in casserole. Combine milk and chicken broth. Add slowly to flour, blending well. Cook until thickened, stirring constantly. Season and pour over chicken and vegetables in casserole. Cover with sweetpotato crust. Bake at 350° F about 40 minutes. Serves 6 to 8.

Sweetpotato Crust

1 cup sifted flour
1 teaspoon baking powder
½ teaspoon salt
1 cup cold mashed sweetpotato
⅓ cup melted butter or margarine
1 egg, well beaten

Sift flour, baking powder and salt. Work in mashed potato, melted butter and egg. Roll ¼ inch thick and cover chicken.

Painting the American insignia on airplane wings is a job that Mrs. Irma Lee McElroy, a former office worker, does with precision and patriotic zeal. Mrs. McElroy is a civil service employee at the Naval Air Base, Corpus Christi, Texas. Her husband is a flight instructor.
Aug. 1942 | Hollem, Howard R.
National Archive, Library of Congress

Home Front Rice and Chicken Casserole

1 large cooked chicken
2 cups uncooked rice
1 ½ tablespoons butter or margarine
2 cups milk
2 eggs, beaten
¼ teaspoon salt

Bone chicken and cut meat into 1 inch pieces. Boil rice in salted water until tender. Drain. Stir in butter, milk, eggs, and salt. Place a layer in greased casserole, then the chicken, then another of rice. Bake at 350° F until well browned, 20 to 25 minutes. Serves 10.

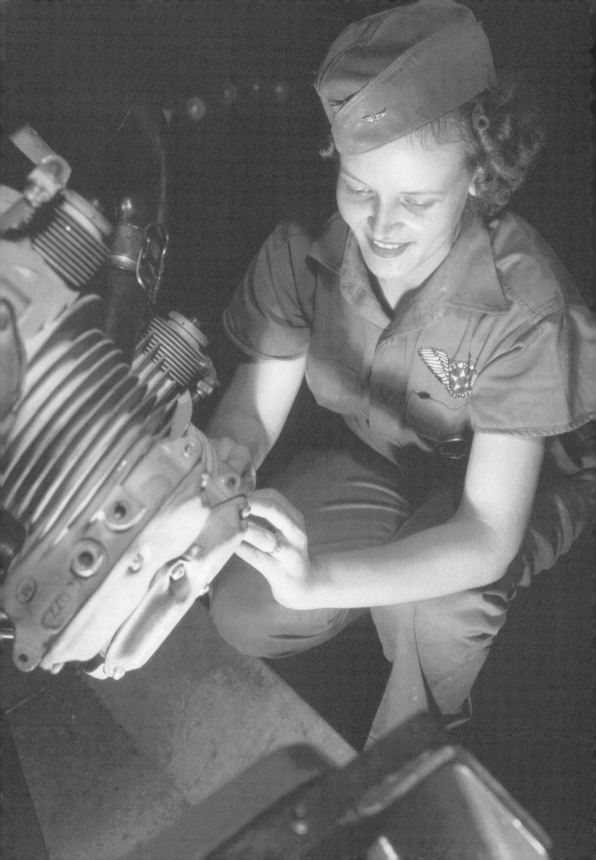

Victory Boiled Chicken, with Gravy

Makes 3 Ration-Free Dinners!

This is a very useful recipe as it can be used to prepare two or three ration-free dinners, each entirely different from the others. It also gives lots of chicken fat which can be used for making biscuits and pastry and is good for cooking other dishes.

Boil one large chicken. Do not cut up the bird, only clean thoroughly. Place in a large pot with enough water just to cover. Add salt, 2 teaspoons to each quart of water. Cover pot with lid and allow to boil slowly until bird is thoroughly tender, about 3 to 4 hours; then remove the bird and make the gravy. There will be a lot of fat at the top of the liquid; some of this is used to make the gravy (more of it is used to make risotto). Be careful to skim off fat only for making gravy. Flour will not mix in well if liquid is present. After making the gravy, chill the balance of the liquid and remove the hard fat from surface.

Assembly and Repairs Dept. mechanic Mary Josephine Farley works on a Wright Whirlwind motor, Naval Air Base, Corpus Christi, Texas.
Aug. 1942 | Hollem, Howard R.
National Archive, Library of Congress

Gravy Recipe for Boiled Chicken
(Dinner #1 from Boiled Chicken recipe)

7 tablespoons chicken fat
7 tablespoons flour
7 cups liquid that chicken was boiled in
¾ to 1 teaspoon grated nutmeg
2 rounded tablespoons finely chopped parsley
1 tablespoon lemon juice
Salt and pepper to taste (remember chicken was salted)

Melt chicken fat and add equal amount of flour. Stir to mix thoroughly with no lumps. Then add seven cups of liquid. Place over moderate heat and stir constantly until the liquid boils; add nutmeg, parsley, and taste for seasoning. Allow gravy to simmer slowly for 10 to 15 minutes. Then add some of the chicken, removed from the bones, and when the chicken is hot add lemon juice, stir and serve. Serve with potatoes or noodles.

Chicken a la King
(Dinner #2 from Boiled Chicken recipe)

White meat from Boiled Chicken recipe.
Cream Sauce (White sauce)
3 tablespoons chicken fat, butter or margarine
3 tablespoons flour
½ teaspoon salt
Dash white pepper
2 cups milk (1 pint)

Melt fat and add flour, mixing thoroughly. When flour is mixed add milk, salt and pepper. Place the saucepan over low heat and stir constantly until the sauce starts to boil. Boil for about 2 minutes, stirring all the time.

Add to the sauce boiled chicken that has been cut into small pieces. Can also add some mushrooms that have been fried slightly in fat for slight variation.

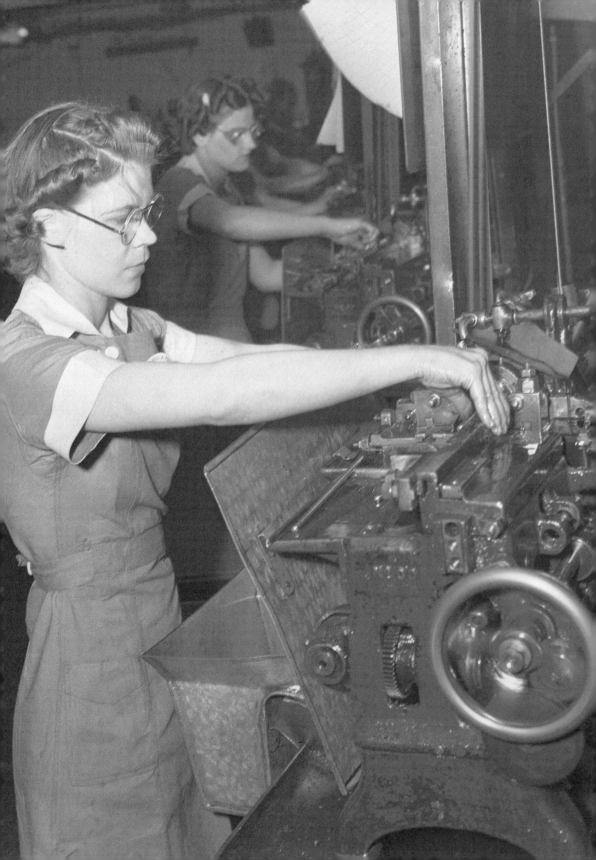

Chicken Kinda Risotto Alla Milanese
(Dinner #3 from Boiled Chicken recipe)

1 – 1 ½ pounds of chicken meat from Boiled Chicken recipe (use dark meat)
1 quart of water that chicken was boiled in, approx.
1 large onion, diced
4 tablespoons chicken fat
1 can tomato soup
1 cup Arborio rice
½ tablespoon paprika
½ cup freshly grated Parmesan cheese
Salt and pepper to taste

In a large pot or frying pan, melt the fat. Add diced onion and cook slowly until soft and golden in color. When onion is golden, add dry rice (do not wash the rice). Turn the rice over and over, slowly to allow it to become heated. Then start adding the liquid in which the chicken was cooked. Add 1 cup at a time to the rice and onion mixture, turning the mixture over and over to prevent sticking to the bottom of the pan. When the rice absorbs the liquid, add more, making sure to add a little at a time. Then gradually add the can of tomato soup. Keep stirring the rice and adding liquid until the risotto is cooked. The risotto is done when the rice has just a very slight trace of hardness. Make sure to taste for seasoning. The rice should not be mushy. Additionally, the risotto should be very moist and not dry. Serve with grated Parmesan cheese.

Women in industry. Tool production. Arms for the love of America! The capable young woman whose strong hands guide this cutoff machine is one of a Midwest drill and tool factory's many women employees. Almost 1,000 women have recently been employed in this comparatively new plant; sole men workers, other than foreman, are those in the heat treating department. Republic Drill and Tool Company, Chicago, Illinois.
Aug. 1942 | Rosener, Ann
National Archive, Library of Congress

Chicken in Paprika Cream

1 five pound chicken
Salt and pepper
½ pound onion, chopped fine
1 tablespoon paprika
1 cup tomato puree
½ cup sour cream

Cut up chicken. Season with salt and pepper. Fry onions with paprika in fat until light and yellow. Add tomato puree and simmer for a few minutes. Add sour cream. Place chicken in deep baking dish. Pour sauce over chicken and bake in oven at 350° F for two hours or more. Shake it occasionally. Strain sauce before serving. If too thick, add chicken stock. Serves 4 to 6.

Gist inspector, Mrs. Mary Betchner inspecting one of the 25 cutters for burrs before inserting it in the inside of a 105mm. howitzer at the Milwaukee, Wis. plant of the Chain Belt Co. Her son is in the army; her husband is in war work
Feb. 1943 | Hollem, Howard R.
National Archive, Library of Congress

Meats

Women in industry. Tool production. Trained to catch the tiniest defect in the smallest drill, this attractive, young inspector in a large Midwest drill and tool plant is doing valuable work for the war effort. These drills, used in the manufacture of every kind of war machinery, must be perfect so that America's planes and ships and tanks can be built to exact specifications. Republic Drill and Tool Company, Chicago, Illinois.
Aug. 1942 | Rosener, Ann

Riveter at work on Consolidated bomber, Consolidated Aircraft Corp., Fort Worth, Texas
Oct. 1942 | Hollem, Howard R.
National Archive, Library of Congress

Victory Meat Pie

1 onion, diced
2 tablespoons fat
2 cups cooked cubed meat
1 ½ tablespoons flour
1 ¼ cups milk or gravy
1 tablespoon Worcestershire sauce
1 cup cooked peas
1 cup sliced cooked carrots
3 cups mashed potatoes

Brown onion in fat and add cubed meat. Sear well. Remove meat and onion from frying pan and add flour, milk or gravy, and Worcestershire sauce. Blend well. Grease a baking dish and fill with meat, peas, carrots and sauce. Pile mashed potatoes lightly on top. Bake at 400° F until potatoes are well browned, about 15 to 20 minutes. Serves 6.

Victory Pot Roast

Select about 4 pounds veal or beef (blade bone or round bone shoulder roast or rump). Brown in small amount of fat on all sides in Dutch oven. Add ½ cup water, 1 ½ teaspoons salt, dash of pepper. Simmer covered on top of range or cover and cook in moderate oven (325° F) until tender, adding more water if necessary. Allow 30 to 40 minutes per pound for veal, 40 to 50 minutes per pound for beef. About 40 minutes before meat is done add desired number of small carrots and potatoes; also 6 cut up celery stalks. Continue cooking until tender. Remove to platter; make gravy.

Woman working on an airplane motor at North American Aviation, Inc., plant in Calif.
June 1942 | Palmer, Alfred T.
National Archive, Library of Congress

Fried Apples and Frankfurters

Serve with potatoes boiled in jackets, cabbage slaw – gingerbread cupcakes.
Pare, quarter and core 4 cooking apples. Melt 3 tablespoons margarine or drippings in large skillet, add 1 tablespoon prepared mustard, ⅛ teaspoon salt, ¼ cup honey or sugar; mix well. Put apples in skillet, cover and cook slowly about 8 minutes, turning once. Carefully push apples to one side of skillet. Add 1 pound frankfurters; cook, covered, 5 minutes longer, turning once during cooking. (If too dry, add 2 to 3 tablespoons water). Place frankfurters on platter, surround with apples and pour sauce over.

Canned Baked Beans and Frankfurter Casserole

6 tablespoons minced green bell pepper
2 cups onions, sliced
4 tablespoons of fat
½ teaspoon salt
6 frankfurters
2 dill pickles
4 cups canned baked beans

Sauté bell pepper and onions in fat for about 10 minutes, or until vegetables are tender. Then sprinkle with salt. Cook frankfurters for 5 minutes in boiling water. Drain, and slit lengthwise part way through. Cut each dill pickle into 6 lengthwise pieces. Insert 2 pieces in each frankfurter. Then cut each frankfurter crosswise into 3 pieces. Place alternate layers of beans, frankfurters, and onion mixture in a 2 quart casserole. Bake at 400° F for 45 minutes. Serves 6.

Military Meat Balls

1 pound ground beef
3 tablespoons grated onion
1 teaspoon salt
¼ teaspoon pepper
1 egg
4 slices bread
2 tablespoons flour
1 cup milk
2 tablespoons bacon drippings

Combine meat, seasoning, and egg.
Toast bread slowly until dry and brown. Cover with water and allow to soak
thoroughly. Squeeze water from toast and combine toast with meat mixture.
Shape into small balls, dredge with flour, and brown in drippings. Remove meat
from pan. Add flour to fat, stir until smooth, then gradually add the milk stirring
constantly until smooth and thickened. Place meat balls in gravy, cover and simmer
about 45 minutes or until tender.

Oxtail Ragout

Have butcher cut 2 oxtails in 2 inch pieces. Wipe with damp cloth, roll in seasoned
flour (flour seasoned with salt); sauté slowly with 2 minced onions in 2 tablespoons
margarine or drippings in heavy Dutch oven. When brown on all sides and 1
teaspoon salt, ½ cup hot water, ½ cup dry red wine, 1 tablespoon vinegar, 3 sprigs
parsley, ¼ teaspoon pepper corns. Simmer covered for 3 hours or until meat is
almost tender, adding more hot water as necessary. Add 6 medium onions or 1
pound string beans cut in half and 6 medium potatoes pared and halved; simmer
covered 30 minutes longer or until meat and vegetables are tender.

Beef and Oatmeal Loaf

1 ¼ pound ground beef
¼ pound ground pork
¼ cup minced onion
1 cup uncooked oatmeal
2 ¼ teaspoon salt
1 teaspoon pepper
1 teaspoon dry mustard
¼ cup ketchup
1 egg
1 cup milk

Mix meat and dry ingredients. To this mixture add slightly beaten egg, ketchup and milk. Place in 8 inch loaf pan and bake for 1 hour and 15 minutes at 325° F. Serves 8.

Note: You can use any kind of ground meat and flavoring for this recipe. What makes the recipe work is the inclusion of the oatmeal, milk and ketchup.

Scotch Lamb Loaf

Combine ¾ cup rolled oats, regular or quick cooking, 1 cup milk scalded, 1 teaspoon salt, dash of pepper, one onion grated, ⅛ teaspoon each rosemary and sage (marjoram and thyme are good alternates); let stand 10 minutes. Add 1 pound ground lamb, mix well with fork and shape into loaf in a greased shallow pan. Sprinkle top with oatmeal and bake 1 hour in moderate oven (350° F). Remove excess fat and make gravy. Makes 6 servings.

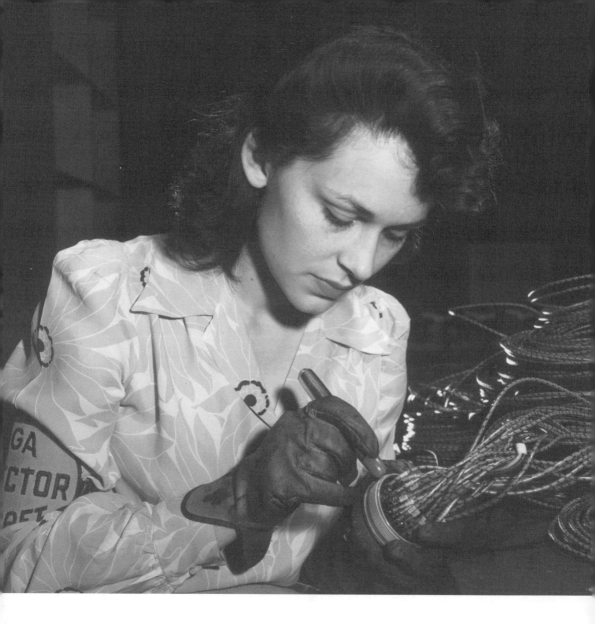

Woman aircraft worker, Vega Aircraft Corporation, Burbank, Calif. Shown checking electrical assemblies.
June 1942 | Bransby, David
National Archive, Library of Congress

Sweetpotato and Carrot Zimes

1 pound brisket of beef
2 cups hot water
Salt and pepper
5 medium sweetpotatoes, pared and sliced
3 cups sliced carrots
½ cup honey
1 tablespoon lemon juice

Simmer meat in water for 1 ½ hours or until nearly tender. Season. Place sweetpotatoes in the bottom of a baking dish, sprinkle with salt and pepper, add meat and liquid in which it was cooked and cover with carrots. Mix honey and lemon juice and pour over carrots. Cover and bake at 350° F 40 minutes or until vegetables are tender. Serves 4.

Brisket of Beef with Sauerkraut and Dumplings

1 onion sliced
2 tablespoons fat
3 pounds brisket of beef
Salt and pepper
1 ½ quarts sauerkraut
1 recipe dumplings

Brown onion in fat. Add meat well-seasoned with salt and pepper. Add sauerkraut and cover with boiling water. Cook slowly 2 hours or until meat is tender. Prepare dumplings, cut dough into squares and place on top of meat and sauerkraut. Cover pan tightly and cook 18 minutes. Serve immediately. Serves 6 to 8.

Women welders on the way to their job at the Todd Erie Basin dry dock.
1943 | Palmer, Alfred T.
National Archive, Library of Congress

Wartime Chili Dinner

Chili Beans
Select your favorites dried bean. Wash 1 pound of dried beans. Cover with cold water; let stand overnight. Add 1 teaspoon salt; bring slowly to a boil; simmer two hours or until tender. Cool in their liquid; store in the refrigerator.

Chili Sauce
Sauté ½ pound ground beef or pork, 1 clove minced garlic, and 2 diced onions in two tablespoons of fat (omit if using pork). Sauté for 10 minutes. Add 3 ½ cups tomatoes and 1 ½ teaspoons salt; simmer 30 minutes, stir occasionally. Add 1 diced green pepper; simmer until thick; add 1 to 1 ½ teaspoons chili powder.

10 minutes before the meal heat the beans, drain (reserve liquid for soup); add sauce and simmer covered until very hot.

Corn and Pork Chops

6 end loin chops ½ inch thick
1 can creamed corn
2 eggs
½ cup bread crumbs
1 teaspoon salt
¼ teaspoon pepper
¼ cup milk
1 tablespoon minced onion
1 tablespoon minced bell pepper

Brown pork chops on both sides; arrange in a shallow baking pan. Mix other ingredients together; place on top of chops. Bake, uncovered 1 hour, at 350° F. Serves 6.

Men and women make efficient operating teams on riveting and other jobs at the Douglas Aircraft plant, Long Beach, Calif. Most important of the many types of aircraft made at this plant are the B-17F ("Flying Fortress") heavy bomber, the A-20 ("Havoc") assault bomber and the C-47 heavy transport plane for the carrying of troops and cargo.
Oct. 1942 | Palmer, Alfred T.
National Archive, Library of Congress

Odd Cuts

Meat has gone to war—gone to feed our armed forces and allies. But there's enough left for all of us to fare well if you increase your repertoire of meat dishes that include brains, tripe, liver sausage, pigs' feet, bacon squares, and oxtails. February 1943

U.S.N. Baked Beans

1 pound navy beans
½ teaspoon ginger
½ cup chili sauce
1 teaspoon dry mustard
2 tablespoons molasses
4 pork tails or feet (or ham hocks)
1 tiny onion
2 teaspoons salt

Soak beans overnight.
Parboil meat with beans for about 2 hours.
Lift pork from broth; remove from skin and take from bones if desired.
Arrange meat and beans in alternate layers in large crock or casserole; add seasonings to broth, and enough additional water to bring liquid within an inch of top of beans.

Cover; bake from 3 to 5 hours at 250° F. Beans may be uncovered to brown the last half hour at 350° F. Brown bread may be steamed in the oven at the same time beans are cooking.

Wartime Note: Here is a place for those peculiar looking pork cuts that are rich in vitamins but low in glamour.

Braised Hearts with Buttered Noodles

1 veal heart or 2 lamb hearts
Flour for dredging
Salt and Pepper
¼ teaspoon ground thyme
4 tablespoons drippings
1 tablespoon Worcestershire sauce
1 onion, chopped
1 cup boiling water
½ cup chopped celery tops
Cooked noodles

Wash hearts, remove veins and arteries, and cut lengthwise into wedges.
Dredge in seasoned flour, and brown in drippings until golden.
Add the boiling water, onion and celery. Cover, and bake for two hours at 350° F,
or until very tender. Serve with cooked, buttered noodles to which 1 tablespoon
chopped parsley has been added.

Conversion. Toy factory. These two girls, Stephanie Cewe and Ann Manemeit, have turned their skill from peacetime production of toy trains to the assembling of parachute flare casings for the armies of democracy. Along with other workers in this Eastern plant, they have turned their skill to the vital needs of the day, and in many cases have seen to it that the machinery they used to use does Uncle Sam's most important work today. Stephanie, left, is assembling toy locomotives, driving screws and nuts with an electric screw-driver, while Ann is at her peacetime job assembling locomotive housings to their chassis. Today both girls are working with electric screwdrivers, assembling parachute flare casings. A. C. Gilbert Company, New Haven, Connecticut.
Feb. 1942 | Hollem, Howard R.
National Archive, Library of Congress

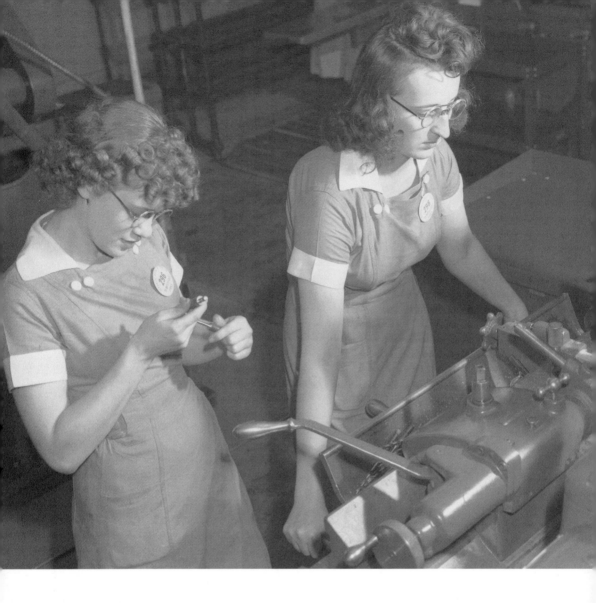

Women in industry. Tool production. Two to a machine, these young employees of a Midwest drill and tool company are operating cylindrical grinders. This work is delicate and difficult, for the drills must be tapered accurately to size. The drills will be used in manufacture of guns, ships, tanks and in all war production where metal must be worked. Republic Drill and Tool Company, Chicago, Illinois.
Aug. 1942 | Rosener, Ann
National Archive, Library of Congress

Braised Sweetbreads

2 pair calves' sweetbreads
2 quarts boiling water
2 ¾ teaspoon salt
2 tablespoons vinegar
4 peppercorns
3 cloves
1 bay leaf
3 tablespoons butter or margarine
1 tablespoon minced onion
¼ pound mushrooms, sliced
2 tablespoons flour
½ cup water
¼ cup milk
Pepper
1 tablespoon sherry (optional)
3 or 4 slices buttered, enriched toast

Let sweetbreads stand in ice water 20 minutes. Drain; add boiling water, 2 tablespoons salt, and next 4 ingredients. Simmer, covered, 30 minutes. Lift out; plunge into ice water. Drain; separate; remove connecting tissues and membranes. Dry. Simmer butter until golden brown. Add onions and mushrooms to butter. Cook until tender. Stir in next 4 ingredients, remaining ¾ teaspoon salt. Thicken over low heat; add sweetbreads in pieces and sherry; serve on toast. Serve 3 or 4. Served with hot-vegetable-juice-cocktail, asparagus, orange salad, tapioca cream, and tea for a guest luncheon.

Spiced Pot Roast

4 pounds boned beef neck
3 teaspoons salt
¾ teaspoon pepper
1 teaspoon powdered mustard
1 teaspoon poultry seasoning
1 ½ cups vinegar
3 cups water
1 ½ cup minced onion
1 minced, peeled garlic clove
8 tablespoons flour

Have butcher roll and tie beef neck as for pot roast. Combine 2 teaspoons salt, ⅛ teaspoon pepper, mustard, and poultry seasoning with vinegar and water. Add ½ cup minced onion and garlic. Pour over beef, cover, and let stand in refrigerator overnight. Pour off liquid; reserve. Dredge meat with 2 tablespoons flour, 1 teaspoon salt and remaining pepper. Brown meat in Dutch oven or heavy skillet, browning fat sides first. Remove meat. Drain off all but 6 tablespoons of fat. Add remaining 6 tablespoons flour and blend. Add 3 cups reserved vinegar liquid and bring to a boil. Then add remaining 1 cup minced onion and the meat. Cover, bring to a boil, then reduce heat and simmer about 3 hours or until meat is tender. Serve sliced hot with gravy. Delicious cold. Serves 6.

Served with buttered noodles, mashed yellow turnips, chicory salad, enriched bread, lemon ice, cookies, and tea for Sunday dinner.

Pigs' Knuckles with Cabbage or Sauerkraut

4 pigs' knuckles
5 tablespoons salt
1 cup celery tops
1 bay leaf
¼ teaspoon peppercorns (8 to 10)
1 minced, peeled garlic clove
1 medium head cabbage, cut in 2" wedges

Wash pigs' knuckles; then cover with boiling water, add 3 teaspoons salt, celery tops, bay leaf, peppercorns, and garlic. Cover; bring to a boil, and then for fuel saving and better cooking, lower heat, and simmer 2 hours or until tender. Then add cabbage and remaining 2 teaspoons salt; cover, and cook 10 minutes longer, or until cabbage is tender. Lift cabbage and pigs' knuckles from kettle to platter, reserving liquid to use as a base for vegetables or minestrone soup.

Note: 1 pound of sauerkraut may be substituted for the cabbage; add it 30 minutes before the end of the 2-hour cooking period.

Served with potatoes in boiled jackets, horse-radish sauce, enriched hard rolls, cherries, cookies, and milk for dinner.

Braised Lamb Neck with Vegetables

4 double lamb neck slices
2 tablespoons flour
2 tablespoons fat
1 cup water
4 carrots
2 ½ cups cooked green beans
3 potatoes, pared
Salt and pepper

Have double lamb neck slices cut ¾ to 1 inch thick. Dredge these with flour and brown in hot fat. Add water, cover, and cook slowly 1 hour. Cut carrots, green beans, and potatoes into small pieces and place in greased casserole. Season. Place lamb neck slices on top. Pour liquid from neck slices into casserole, cover, and place in oven at 300° F. Cook until vegetables are tender, about 30 minutes. Serves 4.

Women are contributing their skills to the nation's needs by keeping our country's planes in top-notch fighting condition, Corpus Christi, Texas. Wife of a disabled World War I veteran, Mrs. Cora Ann Bowen (left) works as a cowler at the Naval Air Base. Mrs. Eloise J. Ellis is a senior supervisor in the Assembly and Repairs
department.
Aug. 1942 | Hollem, Howard R.
National Archive, Library of Congress

One of the girls of Vilter [Manufacturing] Co. filing small gun parts, Milwaukee, Wisc. One brother in
Coast Guard, one going to Army.
Feb. 1943 | Hollem, Howard R.
National Archive, Library of Congress

Vegetables

★ ★ ★

Bantam, Connecticut. In the basement of the town firehouse is the bowling alley, revenue from which helps to support the town's volunteer fire companies. Each night is alloted to a specific group, and there are several hot rivalries. Among the women shown here is Mrs. Winfield Peterson whose husband is foreman of the Warren McArthur experimental shop.
Jan. 1942 | Hollem, Howard R.
National Archive, Library of Congress

Wartime Wilted Spinach

4 tablespoons fat
1 small onion, chopped
½ cup vinegar
1 bunch spinach

Heat 4 tablespoons of fat (either bacon or beef drippings) in a heavy frying pan.
Add one small chopped onion. Cook until onion turns yellow, then add ½ cup of
vinegar. When this mixture starts to boil, pour it over spinach which has already
been washed.

Honey Glazed Carrots

6 medium carrots
Boiling, salted water
2 tablespoons honey or sugar
¼ teaspoon grated orange rind
⅛ teaspoons salt
2 tablespoons margarine

Wash and scrape 6 medium carrots, cut in half; cook covered in small amount
of boiling salted water until tender and most of the water has evaporated; drain.
Combine 2 tablespoons honey or sugar, 2 tablespoons margarine, ¼ tablespoon
grated orange rind and ⅛ teaspoon salt in skillet. Bring to boil; add carrots; simmer
about 10 minutes.

Alternate Idea: Use 3 cups diced cooked sweet potato or 3 cups diced cooked
rutabaga; omit orange rind with rutabaga.

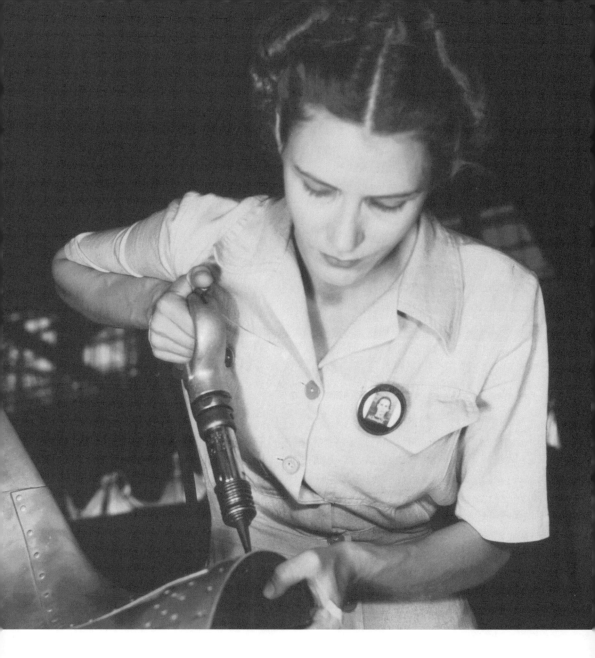

Answering the nation's need for womanpower, Mrs. Virginia Davis made arrangement for the care of her two children during the day and joined her husband at work in the Naval Air Base, Corpus Christi, Texas. Both are employed under Civil Service in the Assembly and Repair Department. Mrs. Davis' training will enable her to take the place of her husband should he be called ...
Aug. 1942 | Hollem, Howard R.
National Archive, Library of Congress

Pan-Steamed Turnips

6 medium turnips
2 tablespoons margarine or fat
½ teaspoons salt
dash of pepper

Pare and shred 6 medium turnips on medium coarse shredder. Melt 2 tablespoons margarine or drippings in heavy pan or skillet that has a tight fitting lid. Add turnips, ½ teaspoon salt, dash of pepper. Cover; cook over low heat about 15 minutes stirring occasionally. If necessary to add water, add just enough to keep vegetables steaming.

Alternate Idea: Cook shredded celery root, carrots, cabbage or rutabaga in this manner, adding a very small amount of water and increasing cooking time as necessary.

Shredded Kale and Beets

½ pound kale
3 medium beets
½ teaspoon salt
Dash pepper
1 cup water
2 tablespoons margarine or drippings
Vinegar and sections of lemon

Wash ½ pound kale thoroughly; with knife or kitchen scissors cut stems and leaves into fine shreds. Scrub 3 medium beets, scraping the stem end; shred on medium coarse shredder. Place vegetables in heavy saucepan; add ½ teaspoon salt, dash of pepper, 1 cup water simmer tightly covered 30 minutes, stirring occasionally. If necessary to add water, add just enough to keep vegetables steaming. Add 2 tablespoons margarine or drippings; serve with vinegar or sections of lemon.

Indian Squash

2 tablespoons margarine or drippings
3 cups squash, diced
½ teaspoon salt
Dash of pepper
1 teaspoon honey or sugar
Small amount of water
2 cups kernel corn

Melt 2 tablespoons margarine or drippings in heavy saucepan. Add 3 cups diced squash, ½ teaspoon salt, dash of pepper, 1 teaspoon sugar and small amount of water. Simmer tightly covered until tender, stirring occasionally. If necessary to add water, add just enough to keep vegetables steaming. Add 2 cups drained whole kernel corn and simmer until heated through.

Mrs. Virginia Davis, a riveter in the assembly and repair department of the Naval Air Base, supervises Chas. Potter, a NYA trainee from Michigan; Corpus Christi, Texas.
Aug. 1942 | Hollem, Howard R.
National Archive, Library of Congress

Creamed Celery Root and Peas

2 cups celery, diced
2 cups cooked peas, and the liquid they cooked in
Milk
2 tablespoons margarine
2 tablespoons flour
½ teaspoon salt
Dash of pepper

Cook 2 cups diced celery root (or celery) covered in small amount of boiling salted water about 20 minutes or until tender and most of the water has evaporated. Drain and add liquid from 2 cups cooked peas (fresh, quick, frozen, or canned) and enough milk to make 2 cups. Now melt 2 tablespoons margarine in saucepan, stir in 2 tablespoons flour, ½ teaspoon salt and dash of pepper; add milk-vegetable-juice mixture; cook until thick, stirring constantly. Add peas and celery root; simmer 5 minutes.

Broiled Green Tomatoes

Tomatoes are delicious when picked green. Slice and broil. Salt and pepper to taste. Sprinkle with basil.

Women wipers of the Chicago and North Western Railroad cleaning one of the giant "H" class locomotives, Clinton, Iowa. Mrs. Marcella Hart and Mrs. Viola Sievers.
1943 | Delano, Jack
National Archive, Library of Congress

Part of the cowling for one of the motors for a B-25 bomber is assembled in the engine department of North American [Aviation, Inc.]'s Inglewood, Calif., plant.
Oct. 1942 | Palmer, Alfred T.
National Archive, Library of Congress

Baked Julienne Beets

6 medium beets
½ cup boiling water
½ teaspoon salt
1 tablespoon margarine
1 teaspoon fresh lemon or lime juice
Dash of pepper

Scrub 6 medium beets reserving tops, if any, to cook as a green. Scrape stem end but do not peel; cut in julienne strips. Place in baking dish with tight fitting cover; add ½ cup boiling water, ½ teaspoon salt. Cook in moderate oven (350°F) 30 to 40 minutes. Season with 1 teaspoon fresh lemon or lime juice, 1 tablespoon margarine or butter, and dash pepper. Makes 4 servings.

Alternate Idea: Cook carrots in same manner.

Beet Greens

Cook these on the day purchased and save the beets for later. The skin on the beets prevents loss of vitamin content.

1 medium onion
¼ cup salad oil
½ cup vinegar
2 quart beet tops

Cook chopped onion in oil until yellow; add vinegar. When hot add beet greens. Cover. Leave on low flame until greens are wilted.

California Style Artichokes

Artichokes
Lemon slices
1 teaspoon salt
1 clove garlic
2 tablespoons salad oil
String

Place a slice of lemon at the base of each artichoke, and tie securely with a string. Place upright in saucepan, add teaspoon salt, clove of garlic, and 2 tablespoons salad oil.

Cover with boiling water, cover, and cook for 30 minutes to 1 hour, until tender when stem is pierced with a fork.

Sauce for Artichokes

Remove, untie, and serve whole with a sauce made of ½ margarine and ½ catsup (sauce is served hot).

Woman at work on motor, Douglas Aircraft Company, Long Beach, Calif.
Oct. 1942 | Palmer, Alfred T.
National Archive, Library of Congress.

Women with no previous industrial experience are reconditioning used spark plugs in a large Midwest airplane plant. Despite their lack of technical knowledge, these women have become expert operators of the small testing
machine. Melrose Park, Buick plant.
July 1942 | Rosener, Ann
National Archive, Library of Congress

Scalloped Cabbage or Cauliflower

3 cups cooked, drained cabbage, broccoli, or cauliflower
1 cup well seasoned white sauce
2 cups soft bread crumbs
½ cup grated or shredded cheese

Arrange vegetables in well-greased baking dish, cover with layer of sauce, then bread crumbs and sprinkle with cheese. Alternate layers until all ingredients are used. Reserve enough cheese to sprinkle over the top.
Bake 25 minutes at 375° F, or until golden brown.

Scalloped Onions

6 medium onions
2 cups soft bread crumbs
1 ½ cups milk
¼ cup butter or margarine
¼ cup grated cheese
Salt and pepper to taste

Melt ¼ cup butter or margarine; add 2 cups soft bread crumbs; mix well.
Peel 6 medium onions and cut into slices ¼ inch thick. Separate slices into rings.
Place alternate layers of onion and crumbs in casserole, sprinkling each layer with salt and pepper, ending with a layer of crumbs.

Add 1 ½ cups milk. Cover and bake in moderate oven at 350° F for 45 minutes. Remove cover; top with ¼ cup grated cheese; bake 10 or 15 minutes more.

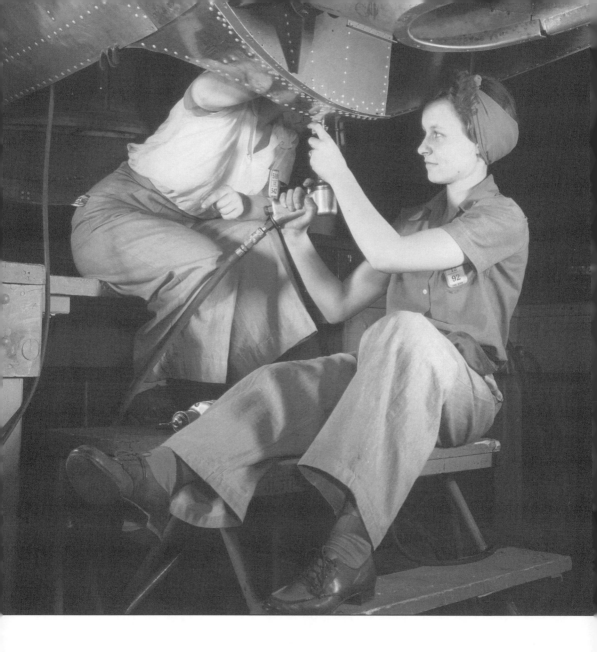

Women at work on bomber, Douglas Aircraft Company, Long Beach, Calif.
Oct. 1942 | Palmer, Alfred T.
National Archive, Library of Congress

Victory Red Cabbage

4 cups sliced red cabbage
2 tablespoons oil or butter
½ teaspoon salt
1 tablespoon grated onion
2 tablespoons water
Few grains nutmeg
Few grains cayenne
2 tablespoons vinegar
2 tablespoons brown sugar

Cook cabbage covered on stovetop, with other ingredients, adding the vinegar and sugar when tender.

Corn Stuffed Bell Peppers

6 large green bell peppers
3 ½ cups whole kernel corn
2 cups soft, day-old bread crumbs
4 tablespoons chili sauce
2 teaspoons salt
¼ teaspoon pepper
2 tablespoons melted butter or margarine

Cut off tops of peppers at stem end; remove the seeds and fibrous portion and wash. Cover and simmer in boiling salted water for 5 minutes. Drain. Combine corn with remaining ingredients and use as a stuffing for the peppers. Place upright in greased casserole dish and bake uncovered at 400° F for 30 minutes. Serves 6.

Operating a hand drill at Vultee-Nashville, woman is working on a "Vengeance" dive bomber, Tennessee. Feb. 1943 | Palmer, Alfred T.
National Archive, Library of Congress

Stuffed Baked Summer Squash

6 medium size summer squash, steamed until just tender
2 cups day-old bread cubes
3 tablespoons grated onion
1 teaspoon salt
½ teaspoon thyme or sage
½ teaspoon pepper
2 tablespoons butter or margarine
¼ cup grated cheese

Split squash lengthwise, remove center and mash.

Wilt onion in margarine on stovetop until lightly brown, then add mashed squash, bread and seasonings. Blend thoroughly.

Re-fill cavity with stuffing and sprinkle lightly with grated cheese.
Bake at 375° F until delicately browned.

Savory Victory Vegetable Sauce

A variety sauce for any vegetable.

Sauté 2 tablespoons minced onion in 2 tablespoons margarine or drippings 5 minutes; add ½ cup fine soft bread crumbs, sauté until light brown. Add 1 cup milk, ½ teaspoon salt, dash pepper and possibly pinch of marjoram and thyme; simmer 10 minutes stirring frequently. Serve over cooked carrots, green beans, broccoli, cabbage, diced turnip, beets and celery root. Makes 1 cup sauce. Also excellent as a variation of white sauce with leftovers, combination meat and vegetable dishes.

The more WOMEN at work the sooner we WIN!

WOMEN ARE NEEDED ALSO AS:

FARM WORKERS	WAITRESSES	TIMEKEEPERS	LAUNDRESSES
TYPISTS	BUS DRIVERS	ELEVATOR OPERATORS	TEACHERS
SALESPEOPLE	TAXI DRIVERS	MESSENGERS	CONDUCTORS

—and in hundreds of other war jobs!

SEE YOUR LOCAL U.S. EMPLOYMENT SERVICE

OWI Poster No. 59. Additional copies may be obtained upon request from the Division of Public Inquiries, Office of War Information, Washington, D.C.

Potatoes, Starches, & Legumes

Potatoes

Victory Twice Baked Potatoes

Potatoes retain their vitamin C when baked.
Wash and oil baking potatoes. Bake in a hot oven 425° F for 45 to 60 minutes.
Once baked, cut into two lengthwise, and remove center, leaving a shell about
¼ inch thick. Mash the potato, season well with salt, pepper, cream, butter (or
margarine), and pimiento (if desired).

Re-arrange in potato shell, cover with shredded cheese, and bake at 400° F until
brown.

Wartime Note: A pièce de résistance when served with creamed meat, or eggs.

*Oyida Peaks riveting as part of her NYA training to become a mechanic in the Assembly and Repair
Department at the Naval Air Base, Corpus Christi, Texas.*
Aug. 1942 | Hollem, Howard R.
National Archive, Library of Congress

Lorena Craig is a cowler under civil service at the Naval Air Base, Corpus Christi, Texas.
Aug. 1942 | Hollem, Howard R.
National Archive, Library of Congress

Volcano Potatoes!

6 large potatoes
2 tablespoons butter or margarine
1 teaspoon salt
Dash of pepper
½ cup milk
6 tablespoons grated yellow cheese
Dash of paprika
2 egg yolks, slightly beaten

Pare, cook and mash potatoes until smooth, add butter, salt, pepper, hot milk and egg. Beat until light. Make into cones about 3 inches high or shape with pastry tube on plank, or greased baking dish. In the top of each potato cone make a deep indentation. Mix grated cheese with paprika and fill each cone.

Bake in a hot oven until cheese melts and browns lightly. Serves 6.

Baked French Fries

Saves your oil ration!

5 pared large potatoes
5 tablespoons melted butter, margarine or salad oil
1 ¾ teaspoons salt

Cut each potato in to 8 or 10 lengthwise strips, ½ wide and ⅜ thick. Arrange in baking pan so that the don't overlap. Pour melted butter over them; sprinkle with salt and bake in a hot oven at 450° F for 30 minutes or until tender, turning them over occasionally. Serves 4.

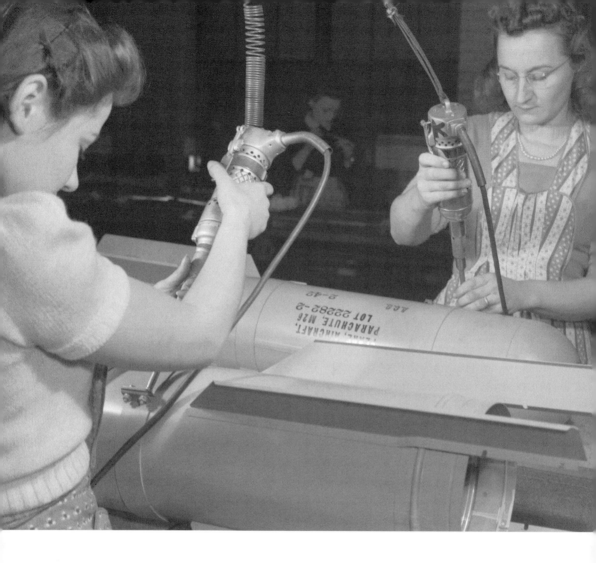

Conversion. Toy factory. Stephanie Cewe and Ann Manemeit, have turned their skill from peacetime production of toy trains to the assembly of parachute flare casings for the armies of democracy. Along with other workers in this Eastern plant, they have turned their skill to the vital needs of the day, and in many cases have seen to it that the machinery they used to use does Uncle Sam's most important work today. Here, they are
assembling parachute flare casings, using the same electric screwdrivers they formerly used to assemble the locomotives of toy trains. A. C. Gilbert Company, New Haven, Connecticut
Feb. 1942 | Hollem, Howard R.
National Archive, Library of Congress

Starches

Kasha of Buckwheat Grain

2 cups buckwheat grain, whole or split
1 egg
½ teaspoon salt
2 tablespoons butter or fat
Water

Place buckwheat in dry frying pan. Add unbeaten egg to buckwheat and mix well. Place over low heat, stirring constantly until each grain is coated and separated, and the mixture looks like a mass of tiny nuts. Place mixture in a baking dish, add salt and fat, and cover with boiling water. Cover and bake at 350° F for 1 hour. Every 20 minutes, add a little water if needed to prevent grains from scorching. Repeat until grains are thoroughly cooked. Serve kasha instead of rice.

Farina Vegetable Casserole

3 cups shredded carrots
2 to 3 tablespoons grated onion
2 cups cooked farina (cream of wheat)
2 eggs, slightly beaten
1 teaspoon salt
½ teaspoon Worcestershire sauce
1 ½ cups grated cheese

Cook carrots in boiling salted water 5 minutes and drain thoroughly. Combine onion, farina, eggs, seasonings and cheese; mix well. Add carrots and mix carefully with fork. Pour into well-greased ring mold and bake at 350° F about 35 minutes or until mixture is firm and top is browned. Unmold onto warm plate. Fill center with hot buttered peas, spinach or celery. Serves 6 to 8.

Legumes

Lentil Croquettes

A nourishing substitute for meat!

½ cup dried beans or lentils
⅓ cup fine bread crumbs
3 tablespoons cream, butter or margarine
2 eggs
1 grated onion
1 chopped pimento
Flavor of mace or nutmeg
1 teaspoon salt and a pinch of cayenne

Place the beans or lentils in cold water and soak overnight. Boil them 1 ½ hours or until tender and then drain. Add bread crumbs, butter, 1 egg, grated onion, chopped pimento and rest of seasonings. Make into croquettes (little balls) and roll in additional bread crumbs, then in second egg that has been beaten. Fry in oil or shortening.

This recipe can be used to make a loaf baked in the oven. If used as such, baste occasionally with oil or butter.

Dhal of Lentils

Take one breakfast cup of lentils. Wash and place into a saucepan with cold water. Boil until tender. Strain and remove from pan. In same sauce pan put a little butter, margarine, or other fat and sliced onions. Add spoonful of curry powder and other herb flavoring and salt while frying the onions. When fried brown, add lentils. Stir well and serve with boiled rice.

Peas Porridge

The following is a good basic recipe for cooked peas. It may be served hot as a vegetable. Serve it cold in salads or sandwiches, with salad dressing, relish or catsup. For soup, thin to the desired consistency with milk, stock, water or tomato soup.

1 pound green split peas
⅓ cup chopped onions
⅓ cup celery leaves and stalk, chopped
¼ teaspoon thyme
1 bay leaf
3 peppercorns
3 cloves
1 teaspoon salt

Soak peas overnight in one quart of water. Add seasonings, onion and celery. Simmer one hour, stirring occasionally. Drain. Simmer again until mixture is of consistency of mashed potatoes.

A good way to add variety and flavor to this basic recipe is to add a ham bone, salt pork, or leftover ham, sausage, tomatoes, or carrots.

Baked Chick Peas

Wash 4 cups of peas and soak overnight. Put on to boil with about ¾ pound of salt pork, one small chopped onion, salt and pepper to taste. Boil for about 2 hours. Drain. Put into baking dish with pork and about ½ teaspoon of mustard and 3 to 4 tablespoons syrup or molasses. Bake one hour at 350° F. Serves 8.

AIR BRAKES

Stuffings & Dumplings

Helen Ryan, age 41 (with cap), widow and used to work in a show factory, Heil and Co., Milwaukee, Wisconsin. Agnes Cliemka, age 23, married and husband may be going into the service any day, brother in the army. [She] used to be a clerk in a department store. Unmasking and checking parts of the gasoline trailers that will be turned over to the Air Force.
Feb. 1943 | Hollem, Howard R.
National Archive, Library of Congress

Stuffings

Bread Stuffing

1 quart dry bread
1 teaspoon salt
⅛ teaspoon pepper
¼ teaspoon poultry seasoning
1 teaspoon finely chopped parsley
½ teaspoon finely chopped onion
2 tablespoon butter or margarine, melted
1 egg
Giblets of fowl or pork or liver sausage

Soak bread in cold water and squeeze dry. Season with the next 5 ingredients. Add melted butter and egg and mix thoroughly. Add giblets which have been chopped fine and simmered until nearly tender. Will fill a 3 to 4 pound bird.

Mrs. Eloise J. Ellis, senior supervisor in the Assembly and Repairs Dept. of the Naval Air Base, talking with one of the men, Corpus Christi, Texas.
Aug. 1942 | Hollem, Howard R.
National Archive, Library of Congress

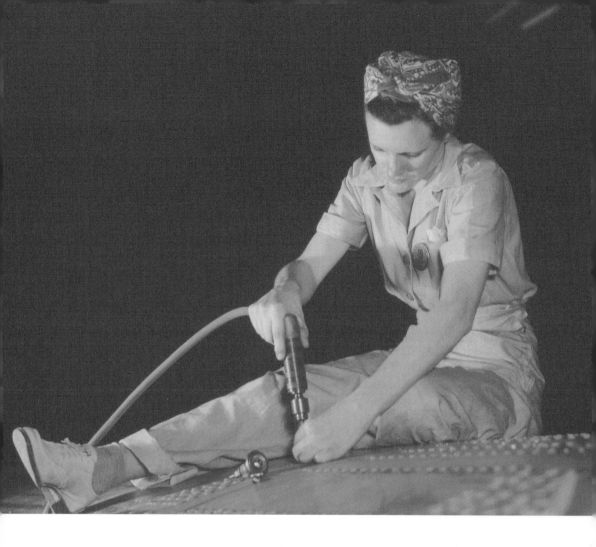

Drilling on a Liberator Bomber, Consolidated Aircraft Corp., Fort Worth, Texas.
Oct. 1942 | Hollem, Howard R.
National Archive, Library of Congress

Apricot Stuffing

½ pound dried apricots
2 cups bread crumbs
¼ cup cracker crumbs
1 ½ teaspoons salt
¼ teaspoon paprika
¼ cup chopped celery
1 tablespoon minced parsley
4 tablespoons butter or margarine, melted

Wash apricots, cover with cold water and cook until tender. Drain (save liquid for making sauces and puddings) and chop apricots fine. Combine crumbs with seasonings, celery and parsley. Stir in melted butter, then add chopped apricots. Mix well. Will fill 4 to 5 pound bird.

Sage Stuffing

3 cups soft bread crumbs
½ teaspoon salt
⅛ teaspoon pepper
1 tablespoon crushed sage leaves
1 tablespoon minced onion
⅓ cup butter or margarine, melted

Combine first 5 ingredients, add butter, tossing together lightly with fork until blended. Will fill 4 pound bird.

Why greases must be saved. Introducing two good soldiers of the home front: the housewife who saves her waste household fats and greases, and the butcher to whom she gives this salvaged fat after she has collected at least one pound, strained it through a metal sieve and poured it into a large, wide-mouthed can. Butchers displaying the poster shown here will pay householders for the fat, and sell it to rendering plants thereby turning this valuable material into industrial channels where it will be processed into ammunition for America's fighting men.
June 1942 | Rosener, Ann
National Archive, Library of Congress

Dumplings

Potato Dumplings

1 small potato, boiled and mashed
Dash salt, 1 egg
6 tablespoons flour
½ teaspoon baking powder

Combine in order given and drop from spoon into hot soup or stew. Cover and cook 20 minutes. Makes 6 medium dumplings.

Egg Dumplings

1 egg, beaten
1 teaspoon salt
½ cup milk
1 ½ cups sifted flour

Combine egg, salt, milk and stir into flour to form a smooth batter. Drop by teaspoonfuls into boiling salted water or stock, cover tightly and cook 15 minutes, being careful not to lift the lid during this time. Drain in colander. These may be served with hot fat poured over them, or may be reheated in meat gravy or stew. Makes 12 dumplings.

There'll be a long wait for new stoves, so take care of the one you own. Whether it operates by gas or electricity, coal or wood, hang this motto above it: Keep it Clean. A little soap and warm water will go a long way toward preserving its life and usefulness. If it's encrusted with grease, use steel wool to clean it.
June 1942 | Rosener, Ann
National Archive, Library of Congress

Irish Stew Dumplings

1 cup sifted flour
½ teaspoon salt
2 teaspoons baking powder
1 teaspoon bacon fat
⅓ to ½ cup milk

Sift dry ingredients, cut in fat and add enough milk to give a smooth drop batter. Drop from tablespoons over top of stew. Cover tightly and allow dumplings to steam 15 minutes without lifting cover.

Conservation of durable goods. That's no idle whim of Uncle Sam's; these empty tubes you turn in before buying more are converted into essential products. Vital tin and alloy metals conserved by this procedure.
Feb. 1942 | Rosener, Ann
National Archive, Library of Congress

Breads

Drilling a wing bulkhead for a transport plane at the Consolidated Aircraft Corporation plant, Fort Worth, Texas.
Oct. 1942 | Hollem, Howard R.
National Archive, Library of Congress

Brown Nut Bread

1 ½ cups graham flour
¾ cups whole wheat flour
1 ½ cups buttermilk
⅓ cup molasses
½ teaspoon salt
1 ½ teaspoons baking soda
½ cup chopped walnuts

Mix dry ingredients, add milk to molasses and add to dry ingredients. Stir well to a smooth batter, adding nuts last. Place in a greased bread pan and bake at 325° F for 1 hour.

Molasses Raisin-nut Bread

2 ¾ cups enriched flour
2 teaspoons baking powder
¼ teaspoon baking soda
¼ cup sugar
½ teaspoon salt
½ cup chopped nuts
½ cup seedless raisins
1 cup milk (or ½ cup evaporated milk plus ½ cup water)
¾ cup molasses
1 egg, well beaten
¼ cup shortening (melted)
2 teaspoons grated orange rind

Sift flour, measure, add baking powder, soda, sugar and salt; sift again; add nuts and raisins; mix well. Combine remaining ingredients; add all at once to flour mixture, stirring only enough to dampen the flour. Bake in a well greased loaf pan, in moderate oven (350° F) about 1 ¼ hours.

A pre-marketing "must": prepare your shopping list by comparing "best buys" appearing in the newspapers. You'll save a surprising amount this way, and those extra nickels and dimes can be invested in other household essentials or in defense stamps.
Feb. 1942 | Rosener, Ann
National Archive, Library of Congress

Graham Bread

1 cup sifted flour
1 ½ teaspoons baking soda
½ cup maple or brown sugar
1 teaspoon salt
2 cups buttermilk or sour milk
2 cups graham flour (can substitute whole wheat flour, but texture will be slightly different)

Sift flour, sugar, soda and salt together. Add buttermilk and graham flour and mix thoroughly. Pour into greased pan and bake at 350° F for 1 hour. Makes 1 (9 x 5 x 3 inch) loaf.

Potato Bread

2 cups potato water (*Cook 3 pared potatoes until tender and mash in liquid.)
1 cake yeast
2 tablespoons shortening
2 tablespoons sugar or other sweetener
1 tablespoon salt
6 to 6 ½ cups sifted flour

Heat potato water to lukewarm. Crumble yeast into ¼ cup potato liquid. To remaining liquid add shortening, sugar and salt. Add softened yeast and ½ of flour. Beat and add remaining flour gradually. Toss on floured surface and knead until elastic. Place in a greased bowl. Cover. Let rise in warm place until doubled in bulk. Punch down. Remove from bowl and shape into 2 loaves. Place in greased bread pans, let rise again until doubled in size. Bake at 375° F 45 minutes, or until bread shrinks from sides of pan. Makes 2 loaves.

"Women in white" doctor Navy planes (motors) at the Naval Air Base, Corpus Christi, Texas. Mildred Webb, an NYA trainee at the base, is learning to operate a cutting machine in the Assembly and Repair Department. After about eight weeks as an apprentice she will be eligible for a civil service job in the capacity for which she has been trained.
Aug. 1942 | Hollem, Howard R.
National Archive, Library of Congress

Rye Bread

1 cake yeast
2 cups lukewarm water
1 cup milk
2 tablespoons butter or margarine
1 teaspoon salt
2 tablespoons sugar or other sweetener
1 ½ cups sifted white flour
5 cups sifted rye flour

Soften yeast in water. Scald milk and cook to lukewarm. Add butter, salt, sugar, softened yeast and white and rye flours. Knead to a stiff dough. Place in a greased bowl. Cover. Let rise in warm place until doubled in bulk. Punch down. Remove from bowl and shape into 2 loaves. Place on greased baking pans, let rise again. Bake at 400° F 20 minutes; reduce temperature to 350° F and continue baking 40 to 50 minutes longer. Makes 2 large loaves.

Old Fashioned Corn Bread

1 ⅔ cups corn meal
⅓ cup flour
1 tablespoon sugar or other sweetener
½ teaspoon salt
½ teaspoon baking soda
1 egg, beaten
1 ¼ cups buttermilk

Sift together flour, sugar, salt and baking soda. Combine with corn meal. Beat egg and add buttermilk. Add liquid mixture to dry. Beat thoroughly. Bake in greased pan (7 x 10 inches) at 425° F for about 30 minutes, or until golden brown. Serves 8 to 10.

Conservation of durable goods. Try this on your refrigerator. Close the door on a slip of paper or a dollar bill. If you can pull the paper out, you are wasting valuable electric power. Have the gasket (the strip that lines the edge of the door) tightened or replaced immediately, and help Uncle Sam conserve electricity.
Feb. 1942 | Rosener, Ann
National Archive, Library of Congress

Whole Wheat Rolls

1 cake yeast
1 ¼ cups lukewarm water
1 cup milk
3 tablespoons shortening
¼ cup honey
1 tablespoon salt
4 cups sifted flour
4 cups whole wheat flour

Soften yeast in lukewarm water. Scald milk; add shortening, honey and salt. Cool. Add dissolved yeast and flour. Knead about 10 minutes on well floured surface. Let rise until light. Shape into cloverleaf rolls and let rise until almost doubled in size. Bake at 400° F 25 to 30 minutes. Makes 24 rolls.

Victory Rolls

Make standard whole-wheat yeast rolls. When dough is ready to shape, roll into an oblong ⅛ inch thick; brush with melted margarine or butter. Mix ½ cup instant whole-grain cereal with 1 teaspoon salt. Sprinkle two thirds of mixture over dough, roll lengthwise like a jelly roll; cut into 1 inch pieces. Place cut side down on greased muffin pans; cover and let rise until light. Sprinkle tops with remaining cereal mixture; bake in hot oven (400° F) about 15 to 20 minutes.
Spread with cream cheese – a dream!

Scotch Scones

Requires no butter, fat or shortening of any kind. Easiest of all hot breads to make!

2 cups sifted flour
½ teaspoon salt
2 tablespoons sugar (if desired or other sweetener)
4 teaspoons baking powder
1 cup milk (sweet or sour)

Sift into a bowl the flour, salt, baking powder and sugar. Mix around thoroughly with a knife; then gradually pour the milk in while you stir until all is combined. This makes a rather wet dough.

Sift on pastry board or table plenty of flour, turn the dough out of the bowl on to the center of the floured patch, using the knife to scrape it out. Sift some flour over the dough and over a rolling pin and roll the dough out to ½ inch thickness.

When dough is rolled out, cut into 10 or 12 pieces, any shape. Place on an ungreased baking sheet or pan. Bake scones in oven at 275° F for 35 minutes. They must be slow baked in order that the dough will raise before a crust is formed. The scones should be white when baked, not browned.

MacArthur Muffins

½ cup butter or margarine
⅓ cup sugar or other sweetener
½ cup milk
1 cup cornmeal
2 teaspoons baking powder
Whites of 2 eggs

Cream sugar and butter. Add milk and cornmeal and baking powder, then beaten egg whites. Bake in a fairly hot oven in muffin pans. Half flour and half corn meal can be used in place of all corn meal.

Cheese Muffins

2 ¼ cups flour
3 teaspoons baking powder
¾ teaspoon salt
⅔ cups grated American cheese
1 egg
1 cup milk
¼ cup melted butter or margarine

Sift flour, baking powder and salt together. Add grated cheese and mix thoroughly. Beat egg with milk and melted butter and pour into dry ingredients. Stir quickly until dry ingredients are just dampened. Batter should not be smooth. Fill greased muffin pans about ⅔ full. Bake at 425° F for 15 to 20 minutes, or until muffins are golden brown. Serve hot. Makes 12 medium sized muffins.

Apricot Bran Muffins

1 cup flour
2 ½ teaspoons baking powder
½ teaspoon salt
1 cup bran
½ cup apricots, chopped
¾ cup milk
3 tablespoons honey
1 egg, well beaten
3 tablespoons melted butter or margarine

Sift together flour, salt, and baking powder. Add bran and chopped apricots. Combine milk, melted butter, honey, and well-beaten egg. Add wet ingredients to dry. Stir just enough to blend. Fill greased muffin tins 2/3 full and bake at 400° F for 20 to 30 minutes. Makes 8 large or 12 small muffins.

Corn-meal Crisps

Mix together 2 cup corn meal, ½ cup enriched flour, ½ teaspoon salt and ¼ teaspoon baking soda. Add ⅓ cup milk and 2 tablespoons melted margarine or other fat. Mix well. Add additional milk, 1 teaspoon at a time until dough just holds together when kneaded. Knead about 10 minutes. Break off pieces of dough, the size of a quarter, roll on floured board into very thin 4-inch rounds. Bake on ungreased baking sheet in moderate oven (350° F) 15 minutes or until browned. Brush with melted butter and sprinkle with salt while hot. Makes 2 dozen. Good with soup or salad. A nice variation is to sprinkle with grated cheese before baking or chili powder after baking.

Desserts

Feb. 1942 | Rosener, Ann
National Archive, Library of Congress

Desserts

Victory Apple Pie

⅓ cup cool potato water
½ cake yeast
⅓ cup riced potatoes
¾ cup sugar
⅓ cup shortening, melted
3 eggs
1 cup sifted flour, about
6 apples
Cinnamon

Combine potato water, crumbled yeast, cooled potatoes and ¼ cup sugar. Let rise 1 hour. Add shortening, ¼ cup sugar, 1 egg, beaten, and flour to make stiff dough. Knead well. Let rise until doubled in bulk. Roll out in 2 circles about ½ inch thick. Place in 2 greased piepans. Pare apples, core, cut into eighths and arrange on dough. Beat remaining eggs, add remaining sugar and pour over apples. Sprinkle with cinnamon. Let rise. Bake in a moderate oven (350° F.) 30 to 35 minutes. Makes 2 (8-inch) cakes.

Conservation of durable goods. Now is the time to take those nice long walks you always promised yourself. Carry those bundles home from your neighborhood stores and thus help conserve tires on your own car and your merchant's delivery truck as well.
Feb. 1942 | Rosener, Ann
National Archive, Library of Congress

War production workers at the Vilter [Manufacturing] Company making M5 and M7 guns for the U.S. Army, Milwaukee, Wis. Ex-housewife, age 24, filing small parts. Her husband and brother are in the armed service

Feb. 1943 | Hollem, Howard R.

National Archive, Library of Congress

Victory Baked Custard

1 quart milk
4 eggs
½ cup honey
⅛ teaspoon salt
Flavoring

Scald milk. Beat eggs lightly. To eggs add sugar and flavoring. Add egg mixture to milk, strain. Pour into cups. Place in pan of hot water. Bake at 325° F for 45 minutes or until knife is clean when custard is tested.

Red Cross Bread Pudding

1 quart milk
2 cups fine dry bread crumbs
2 tablespoons melted butter or fat
1 cup light corn syrup
3 eggs, separated
1 teaspoon vanilla
1 cup jellied cranberry sauce
6 tablespoons sugar or other sweetener

Pour milk over bread crumbs. Mix well. Blend melted butter with syrup and add well-beaten egg yolks and vanilla. Combine butter mixture with milk-bread mixture. Turn into well greased baking dish and bake at 325° F until firm. Remove from oven and spread a generous amount of cranberry sauce over pudding, Beat egg whites until frothy. Beat in sugar gradually until whites hold soft peaks. Spread egg whites over cranberry sauce. Place back in oven and bake 15 more minutes or until meringue is lightly browned. Serve warm. Serves 6.

Caramel Pudding

¾ cup brown sugar
⅛ teaspoon salt
3 cups milk
3 tablespoons cornstarch
2 egg yolks, beaten
2 tablespoons butter or fat
1 teaspoon vanilla

Melt brown sugar and salt in pan over low heat; brown. Add 2 ½ cups milk gradually. The sugar may form into hard lumps but continue heating and stirring until dissolved. Mix cornstarch with remaining milk, add to hot mixture and cook until thickened, stirring constantly. Add egg yolks, cook 2 minutes, add butter and vanilla, mix well and chill. Serves 8.

Homefront Honey Rice

1 cup uncooked rice
¼ cup honey
½ cup raisins
1 tablespoon butter or margarines
1 tablespoon lemon juice
1 teaspoon vanilla
¼ cup chopped nuts
Cinnamon

Wash rice thoroughly and cook in boiling salted water until tender. Drain. Heat honey in a heavy pan, add rice and raisins and cook about 5 minutes. Pour mixture into a well-greased shallow baking dish and dot with butter or margarine. Bake at 350° F until golden brown. Remove from oven and stir in lemon juice and vanilla. Sprinkle with chopped nuts and cinnamon. Serves 8.

Patriotic Rennet-Custard

2 cups milk
1 package vanilla rennet powder
Candied cherries, chopped fine
3 ounces cream cheese
1 ⅓ cups red jelly

Heat milk slowly, stirring constantly. When warm (120° F), not hot, remove from heat. Stir powder into milk until dissolved. Pour at once (while still liquid) into individual dessert glasses containing ½ tablespoon cherries. Do not move until firm, about 10 minutes. Chill. Before serving, decorate with cream cheese and red jelly pressed through pastry tube into narrow stripes and tiny stars, forming a flag. Serves 4 or 5. Can substitute whipped cream from cream cheese.

Holland Truffles

1 cup powdered cocoa
2 cups powdered sugar
¾ cup margarine
4 teaspoons coffee extract
4 tablespoons water

Combine all ingredients in double boiler. Stir and cook over the boiling water until melted and smooth, about 10 minutes. Pour into greased pan. When firm, cut in ¾ inch squares and roll in a combination of 1 part cocoa and 2 parts granulated sugar. This recipe is not satisfactory in hot weather.

Cakes

Victory Honey Cake

½ cup shortening
3 eggs, separated
1 cup honey
½ teaspoon cinnamon
½ teaspoon ground ginger
¼ teaspoon nutmeg
¼ teaspoon ground clove
½ teaspoon salt
4 cups sifted cake flour
1 teaspoon baking soda
1 cup water
1 cup chopped nuts

Cream the shortening until very fluffy and add beaten egg yolks. Mix well. Blend in the honey. Soft dry ingredients together and add alternately with water to the first mixture. Beat well. Fold in stiffly beaten egg whites. Add chopped nuts. Pour into well-greased loaf pan and bake at 350° F for approximately 40 minutes. Makes 1 (10 x 12 inch cake)

Production. Aircraft engines. She used to be a librarian, now she inspects aircraft parts. Prior to Alma Jean Vincent's employment in a large Midwestern aircraft plant, she managed the junior book section of a suburban library. She had also been an assistant buyer of sportswear, but this lack of industrial experience seems to have been no handicap for her present job of visual gauge operator, inspecting airplane motor parts. With only six months of war work behind her, she's more than meeting plant requirements for speed and precision. Melrose Park, Buick plant.
July 1942 | Rosener, Ann
National Archive, Library of Congress

Production. Aircraft engines. Woman's place is on the inspection line in this Midwest aircraft plant where increasing numbers of young girls are being employed for this exacting work. Frances Busch and Lorraine Onobato put in five full days a week inspecting and gauging oil pipes for airplane engines. Melrose Park, Buick plant.
July 1942 | Rosener, Ann
National Archive, Library of Congress

Maple Syrup Gingerbread

1 cup maple syrup
1 cup sour cream
1 egg, well beaten
2 ⅓ cups sifted flour
1 teaspoon baking soda
1 ½ teaspoons ground ginger
½ teaspoon salt
4 tablespoons melted shortening

Blend maple syrup, sour cream and egg together. Sift dry ingredients and stir into liquid, beating well. Add shortening and beat thoroughly. Pour into paper-lined oblong baking pan and bake at 350° F for approximately 30 minutes. Serves 8 to 10.

Everyday Cake

2 ¼ cups sifted cake flour
2 ¼ teaspoon baking powder
¼ teaspoon salt
½ cup shortening
2 teaspoons orange rind
1 cup light corn syrup
2 eggs, unbeaten
½ cup orange juice or milk

Sift flour, baking powder and salt together. In separate bowl, cream shortening with orange rind; add syrup gradually, beating well after each additional. Add ¼ of flour mixture and beat until smooth and well blended. Add eggs, 1 at a time, beating well after each addition. Add remaining flour alternately with orange juice, beating very well after each addition. For best results, beat cake very well at each stage of mixing. Bake in 2 greased (8-inch) pans at 375° F for 30 minutes.

"How do I look?" Attractive playsuits for daughter can be made from that old housedress with the splitting seams, and junior's first long pants (no cuffs) can be cut from father's old overcoat. With shortage of wool and other materials needed by the armed forces, it's a wise mother who conserves clothing by altering and remodelling used garments for other members of the family.
Feb. 1942 | Rosener, Ann
National Archive, Library of Congress

Wartime Spongecake

1 ½ cups light corn syrup
5 eggs, separated
1 tablespoon lemon juice
1 teaspoon vanilla
1 teaspoon baking powder
1 cup sifted cake flour
¼ teaspoon salt

Boil syrup to 240° F or until a small amount forms a small ball when tested in cold water. Beat egg whites until stiff, but not dry; pour syrup over them slowly, beating constantly. Add lemon juice and vanilla. Beat until mixture will hold its shape. Fold in egg yolks which have been beaten until thick and light colored. Fold in sifted dry ingredients. Bake in ungreased tube pan at 300° F for about 45 minutes.

Honey Angel Food Cake

½ cup sugar
1 cup sifted flour
6 egg whites
⅛ teaspoon salt
1 teaspoon cream of tartar
¼ cup honey
½ teaspoon vanilla

Sift sugar and flour together. Beat egg whites until frothy and add salt and cream of tartar. Continue beating until stiff. Add honey, a tablespoon at a time, beating in each addition. Fold in flour mixture, adding about ¼ of it at a time. Add flavoring and bake in ungreased tube pan at 325° F for about 50 minutes. Makes 1 cake.

Honey Cocoa Cake

2 ½ cups sifted cake flour
1 teaspoon baking powder
¾ teaspoon baking soda
½ teaspoon salt
½ cup shortening
¾ cup honey
¾ cup brown sugar
½ cup cocoa
2 eggs
1 ¼ cups sour milk

Sift flour, baking powder, baking soda, and salt together. Cream shortening, honey and sugar until fluffy. Add cocoa to shortening mixture and stir well. To shortening mixture add eggs, 1 at a time, stirring vigorously. In small amount add dry ingredients to shortening mixture alternating with sour milk. Pour into greased layer pans and bake at 375° F for 40 minutes. Makes 3 (8-inch) layers or 2 (7 ½ x 11 inch) cakes.

Women in industry. Tool production. "X" marks the kind of work being done by these women cutoff machine operators who are processing small machine parts in a Midwest drill and tool plant. Although this work is relatively unskilled, industrial experience was new to most of the women, many of whom had previously been waitresses, schoolteachers, or saleswomen. Republic Drill and Tool Company, Chicago, Illinois.
Aug. 1942 | Rosener, Ann
National Archive, Library of Congress

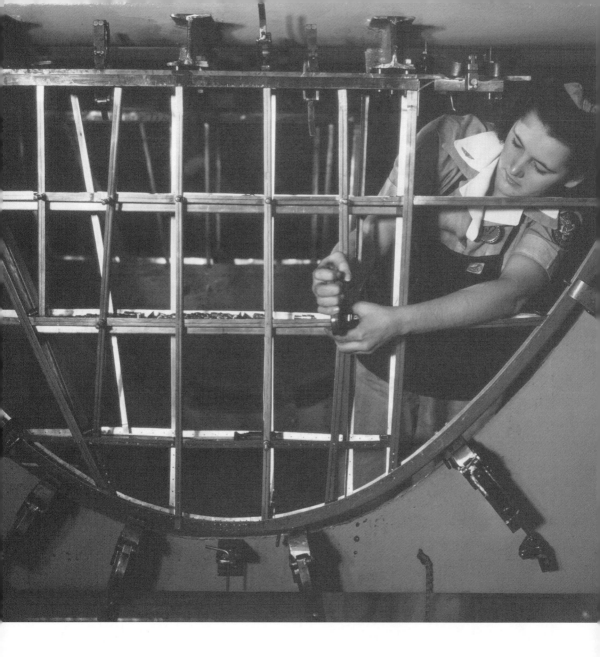

Helen Bray, who left school to become a mechanic at a western aircraft plant, is making an emplanage section on a new Consolidated transport, Consolidated Aircraft Corp., Fort Worth, Texas. This new ship, adapted from the B-24 bomber, is known as the C-87, carries one of the greatest human and cargo loads of any plane now in mass production.
Oct. 1942 | Hollem, Howard R.
National Archive, Library of Congress

Fillings and Frostings

Cream Filling for Gingerbread

1 cup cream cheese
Sweet cream (heavy whipping cream)
1 cup dates, chopped
½ cup nuts, chopped
¼ teaspoon salt

Mash the cheese and mix enough sweet cream to give it a light, soft consistency. Mix in remaining ingredients. Split hot gingerbread, spread mixture between halves and serve immediately. Filling for 8 servings.

Sour Cream Filling

2 tablespoons sugar
1 tablespoon corn starch
1 egg yolk, beaten
1 cup thick sour cream
½ teaspoon lemon or orange extract

Mix sugar and corn starch together and add to egg yolk. Stir in cream and cook over water until mixture coats the spoon. Add lemon or orange flavoring. Filling for 2 (9-inch) layers. Add 1 cup chopped nuts if desired.

Honey Seven-Minute Frosting

1 tablespoon water
1 egg white
⅓ cup honey
⅓ cup sugar
⅛ teaspoon salt

Place ingredients in upper part of double boiler and place over boiling water. Beat mixture until it holds a soft peak. Remove from heat and beat until cool enough to spread. Will cover tops of 2 (8-inch) layers. All honey may be used (⅔ cup) for a very sweet frosting.

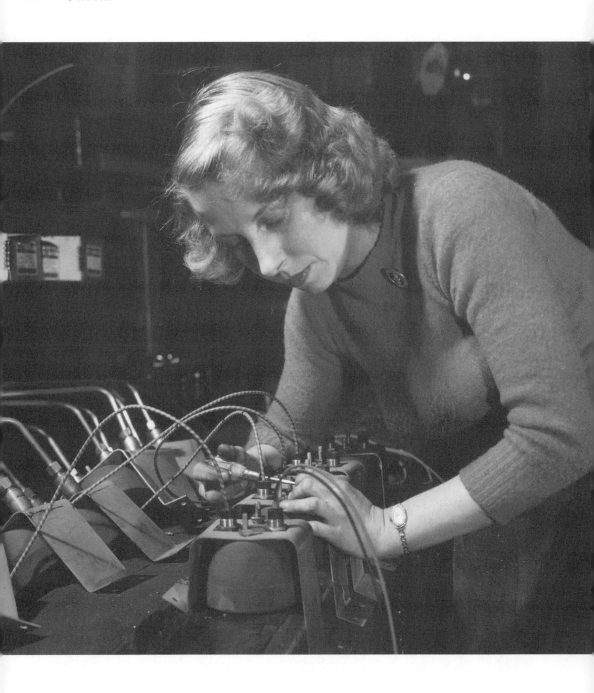

Cookies

Pecan Brownies

2 egg whites
1 cup brown sugar
½ teaspoon maple flavoring
1 cup pecans, chopped
1 cup dry bread crumbs
⅛ teaspoon salt

Beat egg whites until stiff and add sugar and flavoring. Combine nuts, crumbs and salt and fold into egg whites. Shape into small balls and place on a greased baking pan. Bake at 325° F for about 20 minutes. Makes 3 dozen.

Lucile Mazurek, age 29, ex-housewife, husband going into the service. Working on black-out lamps to be used on the gasoline trailers in the Air Force, Heil and Co., Milwaukee, Wisconsin.
Feb. 1943 | Hollem, Howard R.
National Archive, Library of Congress

Honey Cookies

1 ¾ cups sifted flour
¼ teaspoon salt
2 teaspoons baking powder
½ cup honey
½ cup shortening
1 egg, beaten
½ teaspoon vanilla

Sift flour, salt and baking powder together. Mix honey and shortening and add egg and vanilla. Beat thoroughly. Add sifted dry ingredients to wet. Mix thoroughly. Chill dough in refrigerator for 40 minutes. Remove from refrigerator and roll out to ¼ inch thick. Cut with cookie cutter. Place on greased baking sheet and bake at 375° F about 15 minutes. Makes 30.

For chocolate – add 4 tablespoons cocoa to flour.
For drop cookies – Drop unchilled dough on greased baking sheet.

Bantam, Connecticut. Defense homes. The heating unit is in the kitchen of Fred Heath's four-room apartment in the new federally-financed homes for eighty families just a few minutes from the Warren McArthur factory in Bantam. The well-insulated coal fire puts steam in the radiators and provides the heat for cooking. The tenants are well-pleased although on several nights when the temperature dropped to ten degrees below zero they were forced to replenish the fuel every two or three hours. That cigarette Fred Heath holds is not tailor-made, by the way--he likes to roll his own.
Jan. 1942 | Hollem, Howard R.
National Archive, Library of Congress

Maple Sugar Cookies

2 ½ cups sifted cake flour
1 teaspoon salt
2 ½ teaspoons baking powder
½ cup shortening
1 cup maple sugar, sifted
2 egg, beaten
½ teaspoon lemon extract
1 tablespoon milk

Sift flour, salt and baking powder together. Cream shortening, add maple sugar and cream well. Add egg, lemon extract milk and sifted dry ingredients. Mix well. Chill dough in refrigerator for 40 minutes. Remove from refrigerator and roll out to ¼ inch thick and sprinkle with maple sugar. Cut with cookie cutter. Place on greased baking sheet and bake at 350° F about 15 minutes. Makes about 36.

Drilling a wing bulkhead for a transport plane at the Consolidated Aircraft Corporation plant, Fort Worth, Texas.
Oct. 1942 | Hollem, Howard R.
National Archive, Library of Congress

SERVICE ON THE HOME FRONT

★ CITIZENS DEFENSE CORPS
★ CITIZENS SERVICE CORPS
★ AMERICAN UNITY
★ SALVAGE PROGRAM
★ VICTORY GARDENS

There's a job for every Pennsylvanian in these CIVILIAN DEFENSE EFFORTS

PENNSYLVANIA STATE COUNCIL OF DEFENSE
CAPITOL BUILDING,   HARRISBURG, PENNA.

Canteen

Carrot Soup

1 cup onion
½ cup fat or butter
4 quarts water or chicken stock
Salt and pepper to taste
¼ cup sugar or other sweetener
2 quarts mashed cooked or canned carrots (using juice from cooking as part of stock)
1 quart milk

Cook onions in fat in soup kettle until cooked, but not brown. Add rest of ingredients. Thicken soup as necessary with flour diluted in a little cold milk. Reheat and serve immediately. Serves 25.

War production workers at the Vilter [Manufacturing] Company making M5 and M7 guns for the U.S. Army, Milwaukee, Wis. Ex-stage orchestra musician, checking an M7 gun with gage, after turning out on a gun lathe. Her two brothers and husband are in the service.
Feb. 1943 | Hollem, Howard R.
National Archive, Library of Congress

Butterscotch Rolls

Makes 3 to 4 dozen rolls, no kneading.

2 ½ cups milk
2 yeast cakes
¼ cup sugar or other sweetener
½ cup butter or vegetable shortening
2 eggs
2 ½ teaspoons salt
About 7 cups of flour

Scald milk and melt shortening in it as it cools. Stir in sugar and yeast, stir until dissolved.

Add beaten eggs, beat in flour and salt until you have a soft dough. Sprinkle with flour and pat into a ball in the mixing bowl. Cover and set bowl in the refrigerator until three hours before needed. Remove from refrigerator and proceed to…
Generously grease muffin tins with shortening, be sure to grease heavily.
For every dozen rolls, mix one cup light brown sugar with ½ cup butter or margarine. Put a spoonful of the brown sugar mixture in the bottom of each muffin tin.

Shape dough lightly into balls and drop on top of brown sugar mixture in each muffin tin. Let stand two to three hours until doubled in bulk. Bake at 400° F for about 25 minutes. Be careful sugar does not burn. Before removing from oven, have large flat pan ready and turn tin immediately over on this. Lift and let sugar run on rolls.

Conversion. Safety razor plant. Rita Allen sands V-blocks to remove marks made by milling machines. This razor factory has converted many of its machines to the production of tool posts which are essential to war production. Gillette.
Feb. 1942 | Hollem, Howard R.
National Archive, Library of Congress

Victory Bread

1 cup oatmeal
1 lump butter or margarine, the size on an egg
2 ½ teaspoons salt
½ cup dark molasses
1 package yeast
4 cups all purpose flour
2 cups whole wheat flour

Combine first four ingredients and pour 2 cups boiling water over them. Cover and let stand until cool. In ¼ cup lukewarm water, dissolve one package of yeast. Mix flours in separate bowl. Add oatmeal mixture and yeast mixture to flour, mixing well. Turn out onto floured surface and knead thoroughly. When needed into a soft, pliable dough, form into a ball and place in a well-greased bowl. Cover and allow to raise until doubled in size (about 2 hours). Punch down and remove from bowl. Shape into two loaves and place into greased bread pans. Let raise in pans for about an hour or longer. Bake at 450° F for 15 minutes, reduce heat and bake at 350° F for an additional 45 minutes.

Women workers install fixtures and assemblies to a tail fuselage section of a B-17F bomber at the Douglas Aircraft Company, Long Beach, Calif. Better known as the "Flying Fortress," the B-17F is a later model of the B-17 which distinguished itself in action in the South Pacific, over Germany and elsewhere. It is a long range, high altitude heavy bomber, with a crew of seven to nine men, and with armament sufficient to defend itself on daylight missions.
Oct. 1942 | Palmer, Alfred T.
National Archive, Library of Congress

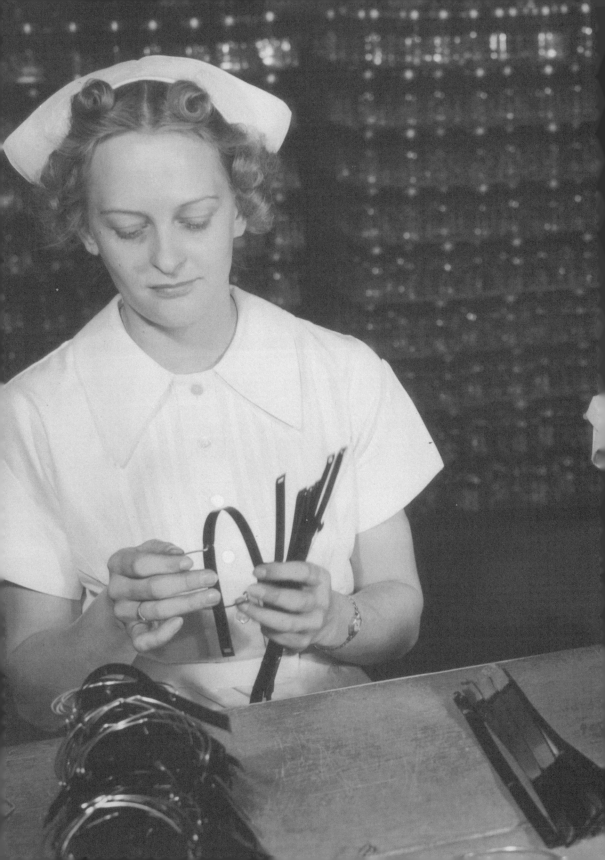

Salmon Supreme

3 cans salmon
1 pound sliced mushrooms, that have been sautéed in fat
4 small packages potato chips
White sauce (made from flour, fat, milk, and salmon liquid)

Crumble potato chips and spread half over the bottom of a large flat pan. Next make a layer of flaked salmon and then a layer of mushrooms. Pour white sauce over this. Top with remaining crumbled potato chips. Heat in a hot oven at 450° F for 10 to 15 minutes or until browned.

Two Navy wives, Eva Herzberg and Elve Burnham, entered war work after their husbands joined the service, Glenview, Ill. They assemble bands for blood transfusion bottles at Baxter Laboratories. Mrs. Burnham is the mother of two children.
Oct. 1942 | Hollem, Howard R.
National Archive, Library of Congress

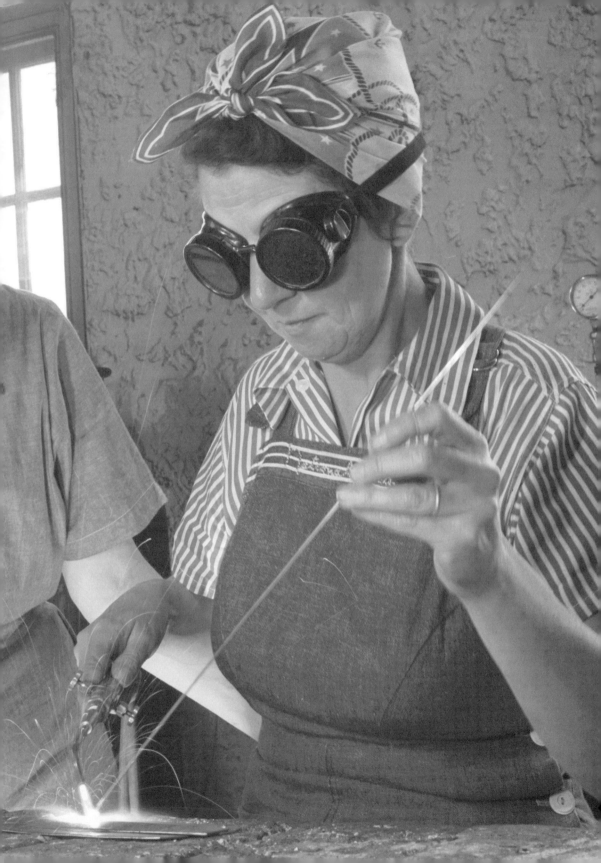

Economy Meat Loaf

5 pounds chopped meat
¾ loaf rye bread, crumbled (use stale bread and soak in warm water. Squeeze dry and add to meat)
3 eggs
1 large onion, chopped very fine
½ cup chili sauce
1 tablespoon salt
½ bunch celery tops, chopped very fine

Mix all together thoroughly, shape into two loaves. Place on dripping pan, bake at 400° F for about 80 minutes.

De Land pool. Aircraft construction class. These two Daytona Beach, Florida housewives talk war work and welding like their grandmothers talked about the weekly quilting society, as they learn to take their places on a war production line in the Volusia County Vocational School. Mrs. Nancy H. Herbert, left, has a son in the Navy. Mrs. Anna E. Larrabee, right, is a grandmother who has one son in the Navy, a second in the Marines, a third in the Canal Zone as a war worker, and a fourth son who is now an aviation mechanic.
Apr. 1942 | Hollem, Howard R.
National Archive, Library of Congress

Vegetable Pie

6 cups flour
12 teaspoons baking powder
1 ½ teaspoons salt
¾ cup shortening
3 eggs, lightly beaten
3 cups milk, approximately
12 cups (approximately) mixed vegetables, cooked

Sift together flour, salt, and baking powder. Rub in shortening with finger tips until the size of peas. Add eggs to part of milk, mix into dry ingredients until mixture forms a ball. Turn out onto floured surface, knead slightly and roll or pat into one-half inch thickness. Cut as desired into circles or diamonds or into one large sheet, size of a pan.

Cover bottom of large flat pan, at least two inches deep with vegetables. Add two or three cups water in which vegetables were cooked, salt and pepper. Top with biscuits and bake 20 minutes at 400° F.

May be served from pan or biscuit turned upside down for vegetable shortcake.

Serve with white sauce, cheese sauce or mushroom sauce.

Don't let pretty labels on cans mislead you, but learn the difference between grades and the relative economy of buying larger instead of small cans. The Pure Food Law requires packers to state exact quantity and quality of canned products, so take advantage of this information and buy only after thorough inspection of labels.
Feb. 1942 | Rosener, Ann
National Archive, Library of Congress

Appendix

Beverages

Barley Water
1 breakfast cup of pearl barley
1 lump sugar
4 lemons, rind and juice only
1 pint boiling water
Wash the barley well and put it in a jug with the lemon rinds and sugar. Pour in boiling water. Let stand for ½ hour, then add lemon juice. Add enough cold water to make 3 quarts. Let it stand for three or more hours. Strain before using.

Summer Herb Drinks
In summer lemon, thyme, peppermint, or pineapple mint enhance the flavor of "store tea". Place a green sprig in the cup and pour in the hot tea.

Mint Punch
Crush a dozen or so sprigs of fresh mint in a bowl and add the juice of 6 oranges and 6 lemons, honey to sweeten, 1 pint of cider, 1 quart of ginger ale. Stir thoroughly, strain, and pour over a large lump of ice in a punch bowl. Float slices or orange, lemon, pineapple, a few strawberries or raspberries, top with fresh sprigs of mint.

Negus
Any sweet wine, although usually port is used. Pour one pint of wine into a pitcher. Add eight cubes of sugar that have been rubbed with the rind of a lemon. Add the juice of one lemon, grated nutmeg to taste, and a sprig or two of costmary (mint geranium). Pour over the mixture one quart of boiling water, cover until cool enough to drink.

Prudent Tips and Penny Savers!
Circa 1943

Time means money, nowadays,
We can all save in many ways!
The things we've never tried before
May be the ones that win the war!

Don't neglect your herbs and spices! Stock your shelf with Paprika, Thyme, Sage, Mustard, Curry Powder, Cloves, Cinnamon, Allspice, Nutmeg, Mace, Ginger; Bay Leaves, Peppercorns, Rosemary; Dried Mushrooms, Parsley, and Celery tops; Chili Sauce, Catsup, Worcestershire Sauce; Onions, Chives, and Garlic. Experiment with new seasonings and develop new and exotic flavors.

• A little wine does wonders for a sauce or gravy that is a bit flat! Use it frequently to give flavor and variety.
• Grind up lemon and orange rind to use for flavoring. The rind contains oil and is more flavorful that the juice.
• Vary the flavoring from vanilla to almond, rose, anise, maple, or any number of others that are on the market.
• A teaspoon of extract is sufficient to flavor a quart of pudding.
• A clove of garlic in French dressing will give it a lift.
• Cheese crackers, crushed fine, will save your cheese ration and make excellent topping for scalloped dishes.
• Try seasoning your pork dishes with ginger! You'll be surprised!
• Sour cream may be used in cooking less tender cuts of meat with superlative results!
• Chocolate, butterscotch, or chocolate pudding mix are delicious filings for cream pies; top with meringue and brown in a slow oven.
• Dip your favorite sandwich in diluted egg and brown on the griddle for the most delectable hot snack you have ever tasted.
• Keep a covered quart jar in the refrigerator in which to store leftover liquid from vegetables. Later, dissolve a bouillon cube and make delicious soup.
• Don't waste those crumbs! Ends and leftover slices of bread may be placed in a slow oven, dried, and then ground up to use for toppings, coatings, and as a filler ingredient.

★ ★ ★

- It's really not so tough when meat is tough! Long, slow cooking will tenderize any cut or type of meat.
- Cold, leftover spaghetti or macaroni are good if chopped and mixed with vegetables, served in lettuce cups with wells seasoned dressing.
- Cream of tomato soup is excellent for seasoning and may save your supply of tomato sauce for other uses.
- Dehydrated soups make excellent additions to casserole dishes, stews, or lean broths.
- Soup bones without meat are ration free, and satisfactory for lean broth.
- Leftover bacon is delicious broken into bits for sandwiches, in chopped apple and celery salad, or as an ingredient in scrambled eggs.
- Fresh fruit prepared in advance for serving should be sprinkled with grapefruit juice to prevent turning dark.
- One tablespoon cornstarch, 2 tablespoons lemon juice, orange juice, or wine is sufficient to thicken and flavor 1 ½ cups of fruit syrup and will make a delicious pudding sauce.
- Make one quart of white sauce at a time, store in covered fruit jar in the refrigerator; heat and season to taste; chopped pimiento, parsley, celery, hard cooked egg and pickle, grated cheese – these are just a few of the possibilities.
- Grind up bacon rind and use as seasoning. Use bacon drippings.
- Cold scrambled eggs may be used in sandwiches, added to soup as a garnish, or chopped and included in a potato salad.
- Outer leaves of celery or lettuce are rich in food value and delicious chopped in vegetable salads, or simmered until tender and used for soup, or in a sauce for vegetables.
- Young and tender cauliflower leaves are delicious dressed with French dressing and served as salad.
- Dry carrot tops in the oven, and crumble into soup for extra flavor.
- Transform your thin meat and vegetable soup into a hearty meal by putting a slice of leftover bread or toast into soup plate, topping with poached egg and pouring in the soup.
- Roll your pattie mixture in buttered crumbs and toast in oven rather than frying in deep fat! Delicious, digestible, and economical of those 5-point fats and oils.
- If you do not have enough eggs for your favorite cake or hot bread, for each egg omitted from the recipe, substitute ½ teaspoon double acting baking powder, and 2 tablespoons of milk.

Index

D

E

F

T

Other Titles From Streamline Press

Streamline Press publishes historically accurate reference books on vintage beauty and vintage lifestyle. We're constantly adding to our library of titles. Collect all titles in the Vintage Lifestyle Series. Ask for them at a bookseller near you.

<u>Available Titles</u>

1940s Hairstyles

Art Deco Hair
Hairstyles from the 1920s & 1930s

Vintage Beauty
Your Guide to Classic Hollywood Make-at-Home Beauty Treatments

Vintage Wedding
Simple Ideas for Creating a Romantic Vintage Wedding

Rosie's Riveting Recipes
Cooking and Kitchen Tips from 1940s America

<u>Coming Soon!</u>

Vintage Candy
An Essential Guide to Retro & Classic Candymaking

Risque Beauty
Beauty Secrets of History's Most Notorious Courtesans

For more information on books from Streamline Press, please visit:
www.StreamlinePressShop.com
or visit us on Facebook at facebook.com/StreamlinePress